The Latest Tower Dual Basket Air Fryer Cookbook

Amazingly Quick and Delicious Dual Basket Air Fryer Recipes for Busy People on a Budge

Fermina J. Reilly

Warning-Disclaimer:

The purpose of this book is to educate and entertain. The author or publisher does not guarantee that anyone following the techniques, suggestions, tips, ideas, or strategies will become successful. The author and publisher shall have neither liability or responsibility to anyone with respect to any loss or damage caused, or alleged to be caused, directly or indirectly by the information contained in this book.

CONTENTS

Breakfast Recipes

Buttermilk Biscuits With Roasted Stone Fruit Compote

Servings:4
Cooking Time: 20 Minutes

Ingredients:

- FOR THE BISCUITS
- 1⅓ cups all-purpose flour
- 2 teaspoons sugar
- 2 teaspoons baking powder
- ½ teaspoon baking soda
- ½ teaspoon kosher salt
- 4 tablespoons (½ stick) very cold unsalted butter
- ½ cup plus 1 tablespoon low-fat buttermilk
- FOR THE FRUIT COMPOTE
- 2 peaches, peeled and diced
- 2 plums, peeled and diced
- ¼ cup water
- 2 teaspoons honey
- ⅛ teaspoon ground ginger (optional)

Directions:

1. To prep the biscuits: In a small bowl, combine the flour, sugar, baking powder, baking soda, and salt. Using the large holes on a box grater, grate in the butter. Stir in the buttermilk to form a thick dough.
2. Place the dough on a lightly floured surface and gently pat it into a ½-inch-thick disc. Fold the dough in half, then rotate the whole thing 90 degrees, pat into a ½-inch thick disc and fold again. Repeat until you have folded the dough four times.
3. Pat the dough out a final time into a ½-inch-thick disc and use a 3-inch biscuit cutter to cut 4 biscuits from the dough (discard the scraps).
4. To prep the fruit compote: In a large bowl, stir together the peaches, plums, water, honey, and ginger (if using).
5. To cook the biscuits and compote: Install a crisper plate in the Zone 1 basket, place the biscuits in the basket, and insert the basket in the unit. Place the fruit in the Zone 2 basket and insert the basket in the unit.
6. Select Zone 1, select AIR FRY, set the temperature to 400°F, and set the time to 10 minutes.
7. Select Zone 2, select ROAST, set the temperature to 350°F, and set the time to 20 minutes. Select SMART FINISH.
8. Press START/PAUSE to begin cooking.
9. When the Zone 2 timer reads 10 minutes, press START/PAUSE. Remove the basket and stir the compote. Reinsert the basket and press START/PAUSE to resume cooking.
10. When cooking is complete, the biscuits will be golden brown and crisp on top and the fruit will be soft. Transfer the biscuits to a plate to cool. Lightly mash the fruit to form a thick, jammy sauce.
11. Split the biscuits in half horizontally and serve topped with fruit compote.

Nutrition:

- (Per serving) Calories: 332; Total fat: 12g; Saturated fat: 7.5g; Carbohydrates: 50g; Fiber: 2.5g; Protein: 6g; Sodium: 350mg

Mexican Breakfast Pepper Rings

Servings: 4
Cooking Time: 10 Minutes
Ingredients:

- Olive oil
- 1 large red, yellow, or orange pepper, cut into four ¾-inch rings
- 4 eggs
- Salt and freshly ground black pepper, to taste
- 2 teaspoons salsa

Directions:

1. Preheat the air fryer to 176°C. Lightly spray two baking pans with olive oil.
2. Place 4 bell pepper rings on the two pans. Crack one egg into each bell pepper ring. Season with salt and black pepper.
3. Spoon ½ teaspoon of salsa on top of each egg.
4. Place the two pans in the two air fryer drawers. Air fry until the yolk is slightly runny, 5 to 6 minutes or until the yolk is fully cooked, 8 to 10 minutes.
5. Serve hot.

Honey Banana Oatmeal

Servings: 4
Cooking Time: 8 Minutes
Ingredients:

- 2 eggs
- 2 tbsp honey
- 1 tsp vanilla
- 45g quick oats
- 73ml milk
- 30g Greek yoghurt
- 219g banana, mashed

Directions:

1. In a bowl, mix eggs, milk, yoghurt, honey, vanilla, oats, and mashed banana until well combined.
2. Pour batter into the four greased ramekins.
3. Insert a crisper plate in the Tower air fryer baskets.
4. Place ramekins in both baskets.
5. Select zone 1 then select "air fry" mode and set the temperature to 390 degrees F for 8 minutes. Press "match" to match zone 2 settings to zone 1. Press "start/stop" to begin.

Nutrition:

- (Per serving) Calories 228 | Fat 4.6g |Sodium 42mg | Carbs 40.4g | Fiber 4.2g | Sugar 16.1g | Protein 7.7g

Sweet Potatoes Hash

Servings:2
Cooking Time:25

Ingredients:

- 450 grams sweet potatoes
- 1/2 white onion, diced
- 3 tablespoons of olive oil
- 1 teaspoon smoked paprika
- 1/4 teaspoon cumin
- 1/3 teaspoon of ground turmeric
- 1/4 teaspoon of garlic salt
- 1 cup guacamole

Directions:

1. Peel and cut the potatoes into cubes.
2. Now, transfer the potatoes to a bowl and add oil, white onions, cumin, paprika, turmeric, and garlic salt.
3. Put this mixture between both the baskets of the Tower 2-Basket Air Fryer.
4. Set it to AIR FRY mode for 10 minutes at 390 degrees F.
5. Then take out the baskets and shake them well.
6. Then again set time to 15 minutes at 390 degrees F.
7. Once done, serve it with guacamole.

Nutrition:

- (Per serving) Calories691 | Fat 49.7g| Sodium 596mg | Carbs 64g | Fiber15g | Sugar 19g | Protein 8.1g

Air Fried Bacon And Eggs

Servings: 1
Cooking Time: 10 Minutes

Ingredients:

- 2 eggs
- 2 slices bacon

Directions:

1. Grease a ramekin using cooking spray.
2. Install the crisper plate in the zone 1 drawer and place the bacon inside it. Insert the drawer into the unit.
3. Crack the eggs and add them to the greased ramekin.
4. Install the crisper plate in the zone 2 drawer and place the ramekin inside it. Insert the drawer into the unit.
5. Select zone 1 to AIR FRY for 9–11 minutes at 400 degrees F/ 200 degrees C. Select zone 2 to AIR FRY for 8–9 minutes at 350 degrees F/ 175 degrees C. Press SYNC.
6. Press START/STOP to begin cooking.
7. Enjoy!

Nutrition:

- (Per serving) Calories 331 | Fat 24.5g | Sodium 1001mg | Carbs 1.2g | Fiber 0g | Sugar 0.7g | Protein 25.3g

Breakfast Sausage And Cauliflower

Servings: 4
Cooking Time: 45 Minutes

Ingredients:

- 450 g sausage meat, cooked and crumbled
- 475 ml double/whipping cream
- 1 head cauliflower, chopped
- 235 ml grated Cheddar cheese, plus more for topping
- 8 eggs, beaten
- Salt and ground black pepper, to taste

Directions:

1. Preheat the air fryer to 176°C.
2. In a large bowl, mix the sausage, cream, chopped cauliflower, cheese and eggs. Sprinkle with salt and ground black pepper.
3. Pour the mixture into a greased casserole dish. Bake in the preheated air fryer for 45 minutes or until firm.
4. Top with more Cheddar cheese and serve.

Red Pepper And Feta Frittata And Bacon Eggs On The Go

Servings: 5
Cooking Time: 20 Minutes

Ingredients:

- Red Pepper and Feta Frittata:
- Olive oil cooking spray
- 8 large eggs
- 1 medium red pepper, diced
- ½ teaspoon salt
- ½ teaspoon black pepper
- 1 garlic clove, minced
- 120 ml feta, divided
- Bacon Eggs on the Go:
- 2 eggs
- 110 g bacon, cooked
- Salt and ground black pepper, to taste

Directions:

1. Make the Red Pepper and Feta Frittata :
2. Preheat the air fryer to 180°C. Lightly coat the inside of a 6-inch round cake pan with olive oil cooking spray.
3. In a large bowl, beat the eggs for 1 to 2 minutes, or until well combined.
4. Add the red pepper, salt, black pepper, and garlic to the eggs, and mix together until the red pepper is distributed throughout.
5. Fold in 60 ml the feta cheese.
6. Pour the egg mixture into the prepared cake pan, and sprinkle the remaining 60 ml feta over the top.
7. Place into the zone 1 air fryer basket and bake for 18 to 20 minutes, or until the eggs are set in the center.
8. Remove from the air fryer and allow to cool for 5 minutes before serving.
9. Make the Bacon Eggs on the Go :
10. Preheat the air fryer to 205°C. Put liners in a regular cupcake tin.
11. Crack an egg into each of the cups and add the bacon. Season with some pepper and salt.
12. Bake in the preheated zone 2 air fryer basket for 15 minutes, or until the eggs are set. Serve warm.

Breakfast Bacon

Servings: 4
Cooking Time: 14 Minutes.

Ingredients:

- ½ lb. bacon slices

Directions:

1. Spread half of the bacon slices in each of the crisper plate evenly in a single layer.
2. Return the crisper plate to the Tower Dual Zone Air Fryer.
3. Choose the Air Fry mode for Zone 1 and set the temperature to 390 degrees F and the time to 14 minutes.
4. Select the "MATCH" button to copy the settings for Zone 2.
5. Initiate cooking by pressing the START/STOP button.
6. Flip the crispy bacon once cooked halfway through, then resume cooking.
7. Serve.

Nutrition:

- (Per serving) Calories 273 | Fat 22g |Sodium 517mg | Carbs 3.3g | Fiber 0.2g | Sugar 1.4g | Protein 16.1g

Breakfast Cheese Sandwich

Servings: 2
Cooking Time: 8 Minutes

Ingredients:

- 4 bread slices
- 2 provolone cheese slice
- ¼ tsp dried basil
- 2 tbsp mayonnaise
- 2 Monterey jack cheese slice
- 2 cheddar cheese slice
- ¼ tsp dried oregano

Directions:

1. In a small bowl, mix mayonnaise, basil, and oregano.
2. Spread mayonnaise on one side of the two bread slices.
3. Top two bread slices with cheddar cheese, provolone cheese, Monterey jack cheese slice, and cover with remaining bread slices.
4. Insert a crisper plate in the Tower air fryer baskets.
5. Place sandwiches in both baskets.
6. Select zone 1, then select "air fry" mode and set the temperature to 390 degrees F for 8 minutes. Press "match" to match zone 2 settings to zone 1. Press "start/stop" to begin. Turn halfway through.

Nutrition:

- (Per serving) Calories 421 | Fat 30.7g |Sodium 796mg | Carbs 13.9g | Fiber 0.5g | Sugar 2.2g | Protein 22.5g

Glazed Apple Fritters Glazed Peach Fritters

Servings:4
Cooking Time: 12 Minutes
Ingredients:

- FOR THE FRITTERS
- ¾ cup all-purpose flour
- 2 tablespoons granulated sugar
- 1 teaspoon baking powder
- ½ teaspoon kosher salt
- ½ teaspoon ground cinnamon
- ⅓ cup whole milk
- 2 tablespoons cold unsalted butter, grated
- 1 large egg
- 1 teaspoon fresh lemon juice
- 1 apple, peeled and diced
- 1 peach, peeled and diced
- FOR THE GLAZE
- ½ cup powdered sugar
- 1 tablespoon whole milk
- ½ teaspoon vanilla extract
- ½ teaspoon ground cinnamon
- Pinch salt

Directions:

1. To prep the fritters: In a large bowl, combine the flour, granulated sugar, baking powder, salt, and cinnamon. Stir in the milk, butter, egg, and lemon juice to form a thick batter.
2. Transfer half of the batter to a second bowl. Fold the apples into one bowl and the peaches into the other.
3. To prep the glaze: In a small bowl, whisk together the powdered sugar, milk, vanilla, cinnamon, and salt until smooth. Set aside.
4. To cook the fritters: Install a crisper plate in each of the two baskets. Drop two ¼-cup scoops of the apple fritter batter into the Zone 1 basket and insert the basket in the unit. Drop two ¼-cup scoops of the peach fritter batter into the Zone 2 basket and insert the basket in the unit.
5. Select Zone 1, select AIR FRY, set the temperature to 345°F, and set the time to 10 minutes.
6. Select Zone 2, select AIR FRY, set the temperature to 345°F, and set the time to 12 minutes. Select SMART FINISH.
7. Press START/PAUSE to begin cooking.
8. When cooking is complete, transfer the fritters to a wire rack and drizzle the glaze over them. Serve warm or at room temperature.

Nutrition:

- (Per serving) Calories: 298; Total fat: 8g; Saturated fat: 4.5g; Carbohydrates: 53g; Fiber: 3g; Protein: 5g; Sodium: 170mg

Cauliflower Avocado Toast And All-in-one Toast

Servings: 3
Cooking Time: 10 Minutes

Ingredients:

- Cauliflower Avocado Toast:
- 1 (40 g) steamer bag cauliflower
- 1 large egg
- 120 ml shredded Mozzarella cheese
- 1 ripe medium avocado
- ½ teaspoon garlic powder
- ¼ teaspoon ground black pepper
- All-in-One Toast:
- 1 strip bacon, diced
- 1 slice 1-inch thick bread
- 1 egg
- Salt and freshly ground black pepper, to taste
- 60 ml grated Monterey Jack or Chedday cheese

Directions:

1. Make the Cauliflower Avocado Toast :
2. Cook cauliflower according to package instructions. Remove from bag and place into cheesecloth or clean towel to remove excess moisture.
3. Place cauliflower into a large bowl and mix in egg and Mozzarella. Cut a piece of parchment to fit your air fryer drawer. Separate the cauliflower mixture into two, and place it on the parchment in two mounds. Press out the cauliflower mounds into a ¼-inch-thick rectangle. Place the parchment into the zone 1 air fryer drawer.
4. Adjust the temperature to 204°C and set the timer for 8 minutes.
5. Flip the cauliflower halfway through the cooking time.
6. When the timer beeps, remove the parchment and allow the cauliflower to cool 5 minutes.
7. Cut open the avocado and remove the pit. Scoop out the inside, place it in a medium bowl, and mash it with garlic powder and pepper. Spread onto the cauliflower. Serve immediately.
8. Make the All-in-One Toast :
9. Preheat the zone 2 air fryer drawer to 204°C.
10. Air fry the bacon for 3 minutes, shaking the zone 2 drawer once or twice while it cooks. Remove the bacon to a paper towel lined plate and set aside.
11. Use a sharp paring knife to score a large circle in the middle of the slice of bread, cutting halfway through, but not all the way through to the cutting board. Press down on the circle in the center of the bread slice to create an indentation.
12. Transfer the slice of bread, hole side up, to the air fryer drawer. Crack the egg into the center of the bread, and season with salt and pepper.
13. Adjust the air fryer temperature to 192°C and air fry for 5 minutes. Sprinkle the grated cheese around the edges of the bread, leaving the center of the yolk uncovered, and top with the cooked bacon. Press the cheese and bacon into the bread lightly to help anchor it to the bread and prevent it from blowing around in the air fryer.
14. Air fry for one or two more minutes, just to melt the cheese and finish cooking the egg. Serve immediately.

Breakfast Calzone And Western Frittata

Servings: 5
Cooking Time: 20 Minutes

Ingredients:

- Breakfast Calzone:
- 350 ml shredded Mozzarella cheese
- 120 ml blanched finely ground almond flour
- 30 g full-fat cream cheese
- 1 large whole egg
- 4 large eggs, scrambled
- 230 g cooked sausage meat, removed from casings and crumbled
- 8 tablespoons shredded mild Cheddar cheese
- Western Frittata:
- ½ red or green pepper, cut into ½-inch chunks
- 1 teaspoon olive oil
- 3 eggs, beaten
- 60 ml grated Cheddar cheese
- 60 ml diced cooked ham
- Salt and freshly ground black pepper, to taste
- 1 teaspoon butter
- 1 teaspoon chopped fresh parsley

Directions:

1. Make the Breakfast Calzone :
2. In a large microwave-safe bowl, add Mozzarella, almond flour, and cream cheese. Microwave for 1 minute. Stir until the mixture is smooth and forms a ball. Add the egg and stir until dough forms.
3. Place dough between two sheets of parchment and roll out to ¼-inch thickness. Cut the dough into four rectangles.
4. Mix scrambled eggs and cooked sausage together in a large bowl. Divide the mixture evenly among each piece of dough, placing it on the lower half of the rectangle. Sprinkle each with 2 tablespoons Cheddar.
5. Fold over the rectangle to cover the egg and meat mixture. Pinch, roll, or use a wet fork to close the edges completely.
6. Cut a piece of parchment to fit your air fryer drawer and place the calzones onto the parchment. Place parchment into the zone 1 air fryer drawer.
7. Adjust the temperature to 192°C and air fry for 15 minutes.
8. Flip the calzones halfway through the cooking time. When done, calzones should be golden in color. Serve immediately.
9. Make the Western Frittata :
10. Preheat the zone 2 air fryer drawer to 204°C.
11. Toss the peppers with the olive oil and air fry for 6 minutes, shaking the drawer once or twice during the cooking process to redistribute the ingredients.
12. While the vegetables are cooking, beat the eggs well in a bowl, stir in the Cheddar cheese and ham, and season with salt and freshly ground black pepper. Add the air-fried peppers to this bowl when they have finished cooking.
13. Place a cake pan into the zone 2 air fryer drawer with the butter, using an aluminum sling to lower the pan into the drawer. Air fry for 1 minute at 192°C to melt the butter. Remove the cake pan and rotate the pan to distribute the butter and grease the pan. Pour the egg mixture into the cake pan and return the pan to the air fryer, using the aluminum sling.
14. Air fry at 192°C for 12 minutes, or until the frittata has puffed up and is lightly browned. Let the frittata sit in the air fryer for 5 minutes to cool to an edible temperature and set up. Remove the cake pan from the air fryer, sprinkle with parsley and serve immediately.

Lemon-cream Cheese Danishes Cherry Danishes

Servings:4
Cooking Time: 15 Minutes

Ingredients:

- FOR THE CREAM CHEESE DANISHES
- 1 ounce (2 tablespoons) cream cheese, at room temperature
- 1 teaspoon granulated sugar
- ¼ teaspoon freshly squeezed lemon juice
- ⅛ teaspoon vanilla extract
- ½ sheet frozen puff pastry, thawed
- 2 tablespoons lemon curd
- 1 large egg yolk
- 1 tablespoon water
- FOR THE CHERRY DANISHES
- ½ sheet frozen puff pastry, thawed
- 2 tablespoons cherry preserves
- 1 teaspoon coarse sanding sugar

Directions:

1. To prep the cream cheese Danishes: In a small bowl, mix the cream cheese, granulated sugar, lemon juice, and vanilla.
2. Cut the puff pastry sheet into 2 squares. Cut a ½-inch-wide strip from each side of the pastry. Brush the edges of the pastry square with water, then layer the strips along the edges, pressing gently to adhere and form a border around the outside of the pastry.
3. Divide the cream cheese mixture between the two pastries, then top each with 1 tablespoon of lemon curd.
4. In a second small bowl, whisk together the egg yolk and water (this will be used for the cherry Danishes, too). Brush the exposed edges of the pastry with half the egg wash.
5. To prep the cherry Danishes: Cut the puff pastry sheet into 2 squares. Cut a ½-inch-wide strip from each side of the pastry. Brush the edges of the pastry square with water, then layer the strips along the edges, pressing gently to adhere and form a border around the outside of the pastry.
6. Spoon 1 tablespoon of cherry preserves into the center of each pastry.
7. Brush the exposed edges of the pastry with the remaining egg wash, then sprinkle with the sanding sugar.
8. To cook both Danishes: Install a crisper plate in each of the two baskets. Place the cream cheese Danishes in the Zone 1 basket and insert the basket in the unit. Place the cherry Danishes in the Zone 2 basket and insert the basket in the unit.
9. Select Zone 1, select AIR FRY, set the temperature to 330°F, and set the time to 15 minutes. Select MATCH COOK to match Zone 2 settings to Zone 1.
10. Press START/PAUSE to begin cooking.
11. When cooking is complete, transfer the Danishes to a wire rack to cool. Serve warm.

Nutrition:

- (Per serving) Calories: 415; Total fat: 24g; Saturated fat: 12g; Carbohydrates: 51g; Fiber: 1.5g; Protein: 7g; Sodium: 274mg

Onion Omelette And Buffalo Egg Cups

Servings: 4

Cooking Time: 15 Minutes

Ingredients:

- Onion Omelette:
- 3 eggs
- Salt and ground black pepper, to taste
- ½ teaspoons soy sauce
- 1 large onion, chopped
- 2 tablespoons grated Cheddar cheese
- Cooking spray
- Buffalo Egg Cups:
- 4 large eggs
- 60 g full-fat cream cheese
- 2 tablespoons buffalo sauce
- 120 ml shredded sharp Cheddar cheese

Directions:

1. Make the Onion Omelette :
2. Preheat the zone 1 air fryer drawer to 180°C.
3. In a bowl, whisk together the eggs, salt, pepper, and soy sauce.
4. Spritz a small pan with cooking spray. Spread the chopped onion across the bottom of the pan, then transfer the pan to the zone 1 air fryer drawer.
5. Bake in the preheated air fryer for 6 minutes or until the onion is translucent.
6. Add the egg mixture on top of the onions to coat well. Add the cheese on top, then continue baking for another 6 minutes.
7. Allow to cool before serving.
8. Make the Buffalo Egg Cups :
9. Crack eggs into two ramekins.
10. In a small microwave-safe bowl, mix cream cheese, buffalo sauce, and Cheddar. Microwave for 20 seconds and then stir. Place a spoonful into each ramekin on top of the eggs.
11. Place ramekins into the zone 2 air fryer drawer.
12. Adjust the temperature to 160°C and bake for 15 minutes.
13. Serve warm.

Gyro Breakfast Patties With Tzatziki

Servings: 16

Cooking Time: 20 Minutes

Ingredients:

- patties
- Patties:
- 900 g lamb or beef mince
- 120 ml diced red onions
- 60 ml sliced black olives
- 2 tablespoons tomato sauce
- 1 teaspoon dried oregano leaves
- 2 cloves garlic, minced
- 1 teaspoon fine sea salt
- Tzatziki:
- 235 ml full-fat sour cream
- 1 small cucumber, chopped
- ½ teaspoon fine sea salt
- ½ teaspoon garlic powder, or 1 clove garlic, minced
- ¼ teaspoon dried dill, or 1 teaspoon finely chopped fresh dill
- For Garnish/Serving:
- 120 ml crumbled feta cheese (about 60 g)
- Diced red onions
- Sliced black olives
- Sliced cucumbers

Directions:

1. Preheat the air fryer to 176°C. 2. Place the lamb, onions, olives, tomato sauce, oregano, garlic, and salt in a large bowl. Mix well to combine the ingredients. 3. Using your hands, form the mixture into sixteen 3-inch patties. Place the patties in the two air fryer drawers and air fry for 20 minutes, flipping halfway through. Remove the patties and place them on a serving platter. 4. While the patties cook, make the tzatziki: Place all the ingredients in a small bowl and stir well. Cover and store in the fridge until ready to serve. Garnish with ground black pepper before serving. 5. Serve the patties with a dollop of tzatziki, a sprinkle of crumbled feta cheese, diced red onions, sliced black olives, and sliced cucumbers. 6. Store leftovers in an airtight container in the refrigerator for up to 5 days or in the freezer for up to a month. Reheat the patties in a preheated 200°C air fryer for a few minutes, until warmed through.

Morning Egg Rolls

Servings: 6
Cooking Time: 13 Minutes.

Ingredients:

- 2 eggs
- 2 tablespoons milk
- Salt, to taste
- Black pepper, to taste
- ½ cup shredded cheddar cheese
- 2 sausage patties
- 6 egg roll wrappers
- 1 tablespoon olive oil
- 1 cup water

Directions:

1. Grease a small skillet with some olive oil and place it over medium heat.
2. Add sausage patties and cook them until brown.
3. Chop the cooked patties into small pieces. Beat eggs with salt, black pepper, and milk in a mixing bowl.
4. Grease the same skillet with 1 teaspoon of olive oil and pour the egg mixture into it.
5. Stir cook to make scrambled eggs.
6. Add sausage, mix well and remove the skillet from the heat.
7. Spread an egg roll wrapper on the working surface in a diamond shape position.
8. Add a tablespoon of cheese at the bottom third of the roll wrapper.
9. Top the cheese with egg mixture and wet the edges of the wrapper with water.
10. Fold the two corners of the wrapper and roll it, then seal the edges.
11. Repeat the same steps and divide the rolls in the two crisper plates.
12. Return the crisper plates to the Tower Dual Zone Air Fryer.
13. Choose the Air Fry mode for Zone 1 and set the temperature to 375 degrees F and the time to 13 minutes.
14. Select the "MATCH" button to copy the settings for Zone 2.
15. Initiate cooking by pressing the START/STOP button.
16. Flip the rolls after 8 minutes and continue cooking for another 5 minutes.
17. Serve warm and fresh.

Nutrition:

- (Per serving) Calories 282 | Fat 15g |Sodium 526mg | Carbs 20g | Fiber 0.6g | Sugar 3.3g | Protein 16g

Cheesy Bell Pepper Eggs

Servings: 4
Cooking Time: 15 Minutes

Ingredients:

- 4 medium green peppers
- 85 g cooked ham, chopped
- ¼ medium onion, peeled and chopped
- 8 large eggs
- 235 ml mild Cheddar cheese

Directions:

1. Cut the tops off each pepper. Remove the seeds and the white membranes with a small knife. Place ham and onion into each pepper.
2. Crack 2 eggs into each pepper. Top with 60 ml cheese per pepper. Place into the zone 1 air fryer basket.
3. Adjust the temperature to 200°C and air fry for 15 minutes.
4. When fully cooked, peppers will be tender and eggs will be firm. Serve immediately.

Turkey Ham Muffins

Servings: 16
Cooking Time: 10 Minutes
Ingredients:

- 1 egg
- 340g all-purpose flour
- 85g turkey ham, chopped
- 2 tbsp mix herbs, chopped
- 235g cheddar cheese, shredded
- 1 onion, chopped
- 2 tsp baking powder
- 2 tbsp butter, melted
- 237ml milk
- Pepper
- Salt

Directions:

1. In a large bowl, mix flour and baking powder.
2. Add egg, butter, and milk and mix until well combined.
3. Add herbs, cheese, onion, and turkey ham and mix well.
4. Insert a crisper plate in the Tower air fryer baskets.
5. Pour the batter into the silicone muffin moulds.
6. Place muffin moulds in both baskets.
7. Select zone 1, then select "air fry" mode and set the temperature to 355 degrees F for 10 minutes. Press "match" to match zone 2 settings to zone 1. Press "start/stop" to begin.

Nutrition:

- (Per serving) Calories 140 | Fat 4.8g |Sodium 126mg | Carbs 18.2g | Fiber 0.7g | Sugar 1.2g | Protein 5.8g

Pork Sausage Eggs With Mustard Sauce

Servings: 8
Cooking Time: 12 Minutes
Ingredients:

- 450 g pork sausage meat
- 8 soft-boiled or hard-boiled eggs, peeled
- 1 large egg
- 2 tablespoons milk
- 235 ml crushed pork scratchings
- Smoky Mustard Sauce:
- 60 ml mayonnaise
- 2 tablespoons sour cream
- 1 tablespoon Dijon mustard
- 1 teaspoon chipotle hot sauce

Directions:

1. Divide the sausage into 8 portions. Take each portion of sausage, pat it down into a patty, and place 1 egg in the middle, gently wrapping the sausage around the egg until the egg is completely covered.
2. Repeat with the remaining eggs and sausage. In a small shallow bowl, whisk the egg and milk until frothy. In another shallow bowl, place the crushed pork scratchings. Working one at a time, dip a sausage-wrapped egg into the beaten egg and then into the pork scratchings, gently rolling to coat evenly. Repeat with the remaining sausage-wrapped eggs.
3. Put them half in zone 1, the remaining in zone 2. Lightly spray with olive oil. In zone 1 , select Air fry button, adjust temperature to 200°C, set time to 10 to 12 minutes. In zone 2, select Match Cook and press Start. Pause halfway through the baking time to turn the eggs, until the eggs are hot and the sausage is cooked through.
4. To make the sauce:
5. In a small bowl, combine the mayonnaise, sour cream, Dijon, and hot sauce. Whisk until thoroughly combined. Serve with the Scotch eggs.

Canadian Bacon Muffin Sandwiches And All-in-one Toast

Servings: 5

Cooking Time: 10 Minutes

Ingredients:

- Canadian Bacon Muffin Sandwiches:
- 4 English muffins, split
- 8 slices back bacon
- 4 slices cheese
- Cooking spray
- All-in-One Toast:
- 1 strip bacon, diced
- 1 slice 1-inch thick bread
- 1 egg
- Salt and freshly ground black pepper, to taste
- 60 ml grated Monterey Jack or Chedday cheese

Directions:

1. Make the Canadian Bacon Muffin Sandwiches :
2. 1. Preheat the air fryer to 190°C. Make the sandwiches: Top each of 4 muffin halves with 2 slices of bacon, 1 slice of cheese, and finish with the remaining muffin half. 3. Put the sandwiches in the zone 1 air fryer basket and spritz the tops with cooking spray. 4. Bake for 4 minutes. Flip the sandwiches and bake for another 4 minutes. 5. Divide the sandwiches among four plates and serve warm.
3. Make the All-in-One Toast :
4. Preheat the air fryer to 205°C.
5. Air fry the bacon in zone 2 basket for 3 minutes, shaking the basket once or twice while it cooks. Remove the bacon to a paper towel lined plate and set aside.
6. Use a sharp paring knife to score a large circle in the middle of the slice of bread, cutting halfway through, but not all the way through to the cutting board. Press down on the circle in the center of the bread slice to create an indentation.
7. Transfer the slice of bread, hole side up, to the zone 2 air fryer basket. Crack the egg into the center of the bread, and season with salt and pepper.
8. Adjust the air fryer temperature to 190°C and air fry for 5 minutes. Sprinkle the grated cheese around the edges of the bread, leaving the center of the yolk uncovered, and top with the cooked bacon. Press the cheese and bacon into the bread lightly to help anchor it to the bread and prevent it from blowing around in the air fryer.
9. Air fry for one or two more minutes, just to melt the cheese and finish cooking the egg. Serve immediately.

Double-dipped Mini Cinnamon Biscuits

Servings: 8 Biscuits
Cooking Time: 13 Minutes
Ingredients:

- 475 ml blanched almond flour
- 120 ml liquid or powdered sweetener
- 1 teaspoon baking powder
- ½ teaspoon fine sea salt
- 60 ml plus 2 tablespoons (¾ stick) very cold unsalted butter
- 60 ml unsweetened, unflavoured almond milk
- 1 large egg
- 1 teaspoon vanilla extract
- 3 teaspoons ground cinnamon
- Glaze:
- 120 ml powdered sweetener
- 60 ml double cream or unsweetened, unflavoured almond milk

Directions:

1. Preheat the air fryer to 175°C. Line a pie pan that fits into your air fryer with parchment paper. 2. In a medium-sized bowl, mix together the almond flour, sweetener , baking powder, and salt. Cut the butter into ½-inch squares, then use a hand mixer to work the butter into the dry ingredients. When you are done, the mixture should still have chunks of butter. 3. In a small bowl, whisk together the almond milk, egg, and vanilla extract until blended. Using a fork, stir the wet ingredients into the dry ingredients until large clumps form. Add the cinnamon and use your hands to swirl it into the dough. 4. Form the dough into sixteen 1-inch balls and place them on the prepared pan, spacing them about ½ inch apart. Bake in the zone 1 air fryer basket until golden, 10 to 13 minutes. Remove from the air fryer and let cool on the pan for at least 5 minutes. 5. While the biscuits bake, make the glaze: Place the powdered sweetener in a small bowl and slowly stir in the heavy cream with a fork. 6. When the biscuits have cooled somewhat, dip the tops into the glaze, allow it to dry a bit, and then dip again for a thick glaze. 7. Serve warm or at room temperature. Store unglazed biscuits in an airtight container in the refrigerator for up to 3 days or in the freezer for up to a month. Reheat in a preheated 175°C air fryer for 5 minutes, or until warmed through, and dip in the glaze as instructed above.

Baked Peach Oatmeal

Servings: 6
Cooking Time: 30 Minutes
Ingredients:

- Olive oil cooking spray
- 475 ml certified gluten-free rolled oats
- 475 ml unsweetened almond milk
- 60 ml honey, plus more for drizzling (optional)
- 120 ml non-fat plain Greek yoghurt
- 1 teaspoon vanilla extract
- ½ teaspoon ground cinnamon
- ¼ teaspoon salt
- 350 ml diced peaches, divided, plus more for serving (optional)

Directions:

1. Lightly coat the inside of a 6-inch cake pan with olive oil cooking spray. In a large bowl, mix together the oats, almond milk, honey, yoghurt, vanilla, cinnamon, and salt until well combined.
2. Fold in 180 ml peaches and then pour the mixture into the prepared cake pan. Sprinkle the remaining peaches across the top of the oatmeal mixture.
3. Place the cake pan into the zone 1 drawer and bake at 190°C for 30 minutes. Allow to set and cool for 5 minutes before serving with additional fresh fruit and honey for drizzling, if desired.

Vanilla Strawberry Doughnuts

Servings: 8
Cooking Time: 15 Minutes
Ingredients:

- 1 egg
- ½ cup strawberries, diced
- 80ml cup milk
- 1 tsp cinnamon
- 1 tsp baking soda
- 136g all-purpose flour
- 2 tsp vanilla
- 2 tbsp butter, melted
- 73g sugar
- ½ tsp salt

Directions:

1. In a bowl, mix flour, cinnamon, baking soda, sugar, and salt.
2. In a separate bowl, whisk egg, milk, butter, and vanilla.
3. Pour egg mixture into the flour mixture and mix until well combined.
4. Add strawberries and mix well.
5. Pour batter into the silicone doughnut moulds.
6. Insert a crisper plate in the Tower air fryer baskets.
7. Place doughnut moulds in both baskets.
8. Select zone 1, then select "air fry" mode and set the temperature to 320 degrees F for 15 minutes. Press "match" to match zone 2 settings to zone 1. Press "start/stop" to begin.

Nutrition:

- (Per serving) Calories 133 | Fat 3.8g |Sodium 339mg | Carbs 21.9g | Fiber 0.8g | Sugar 9.5g | Protein 2.7g

Perfect Cinnamon Toast

Servings: 6
Cooking Time: 10 Minutes
Ingredients:

- 12 slices whole-wheat bread
- 1 stick butter, room temperature
- ½ cup white sugar
- 1½ teaspoons ground cinnamon
- 1½ teaspoons pure vanilla extract
- 1 pinch kosher salt
- 2 pinches freshly ground black pepper (optional)

Directions:

1. Mash the softened butter with a fork or the back of a spoon in a bowl. Add the sugar, cinnamon, vanilla, and salt. Stir until everything is well combined.
2. Spread one-sixth of the mixture onto each slice of bread, making sure to cover the entire surface.
3. Install a crisper plate in both drawers. Place half the bread sliced in the zone 1 drawer and half in the zone 2 drawer, then insert the drawers into the unit.
4. Select zone 1, select AIR FRY, set temperature to 400 degrees F/ 200 degrees C, and set time to 5 minutes. Select MATCH to match zone 2 settings to zone 1. Press theSTART/STOP button to begin cooking
5. When cooking is complete, remove the slices and cut them diagonally.
6. Serve immediately.

Nutrition:

- (Per serving) Calories 322 | Fat 16.5g | Sodium 249mg | Carbs 39.3g | Fiber 4.2g | Sugar 18.2g | Protein 8.2g

Snacks And Appetizers Recipes

Shrimp Pirogues

Servings: 8
Cooking Time: 4 To 5 Minutes
Ingredients:

- 340 g small, peeled, and deveined raw shrimp
- 85 g soft white cheese, room temperature
- 2 tablespoons natural yoghurt
- 1 teaspoon lemon juice
- 1 teaspoon dried dill weed, crushed
- Salt, to taste
- 4 small hothouse cucumbers, each approximately 6 inches long

Directions:

1. Pour 4 tablespoons water in bottom of air fryer drawer.
2. Place shrimp in air fryer basket in single layer and air fry at 200°C for 4 to 5 minutes, just until done. Watch carefully because shrimp cooks quickly, and overcooking makes it tough.
3. Chop shrimp into small pieces, no larger than ½ inch. Refrigerate while mixing the remaining ingredients.
4. With a fork, mash and whip the soft white cheese until smooth.
5. Stir in the yoghurt and beat until smooth. Stir in lemon juice, dill weed, and chopped shrimp.
6. Taste for seasoning. If needed, add ¼ to ½ teaspoon salt to suit your taste.
7. Store in refrigerator until serving time.
8. When ready to serve, wash and dry cucumbers and split them lengthwise. Scoop out the seeds and turn cucumbers upside down on paper towels to drain for 10 minutes.
9. Just before filling, wipe centres of cucumbers dry. Spoon the shrimp mixture into the pirogues and cut in half crosswise. Serve immediately.

Bacon Wrapped Tater Tots

Servings: 8
Cooking Time: 15 Minutes
Ingredients:

- 8 bacon slices
- 3 tablespoons honey
- ½ tablespoon chipotle chile powder
- 16 frozen tater tots

Directions:

1. Cut the bacon slices in half and wrap each tater tot with a bacon slice.
2. Brush the bacon with honey and drizzle chipotle chile powder over them.
3. Insert a toothpick to seal the bacon.
4. Place the wrapped tots in the air fryer baskets.
5. Return the air fryer basket 1 to Zone 1, and basket 2 to Zone 2 of the Tower 2-Basket Air Fryer.
6. Choose the “Air Fry” mode for Zone 1 at 350 degrees F and 14 minutes of cooking time.
7. Select the “MATCH COOK” option to copy the settings for Zone 2.
8. Initiate cooking by pressing the START/PAUSE BUTTON.
9. Serve warm.

Beef Taquitos

Servings: 8
Cooking Time: 6 Minutes

Ingredients:

- 455g lean beef mince
- 1 teaspoon salt
- 70g salsa
- ½ teaspoon granulated garlic
- ½ teaspoon chili powder
- ½ teaspoon cumin
- 100g shredded cheese
- 12 mini corn tortillas

Directions:

1. Season beef mince with salt in a frying pan and cook over medium-high heat.
2. Cook until the meat is nicely browned, stirring frequently and breaking it into fine crumbles. Remove from the heat and drain any remaining grease.
3. Stir in the salsa, garlic, chili powder, cumin, and cheese until all ingredients are completely incorporated, and the cheese has melted.
4. Warm tortillas on a grill or iron frying pan to make them flexible. Allow them to warm rather than crisp and brown.
5. Fill each tortilla with about 1 to 2 tablespoons of the meat mixture and roll it up.
6. Press either "Zone 1" or "Zone 2" and then rotate the knob to select "Air Fryer".
7. Set the temperature to 175 degrees C, and then set the time for 5 minutes to preheat.
8. After preheating, arrange them into the basket.
9. Slide the basket into the Air Fryer and set the time for 6 minutes.
10. After cooking time is completed, place on a wire rack for a few minutes, then transfer onto serving plates and serve.

Dijon Cheese Sandwich

Servings:2
Cooking Time:10

Ingredients:

- 4 large slices sourdough, whole grain
- 4 tablespoons of Dijon mustard
- 1-1/2 cup grated sharp cheddar cheese
- 2 teaspoons green onion, chopped the green part
- 2 tablespoons of butter melted

Directions:

1. Brush the melted butter on one side of all the bread slices.
2. Then spread Dijon mustard on other sides of slices.
3. Then top the 2 bread slices with cheddar cheese and top it with green onions.
4. Cover with the remaining two slices to make two sandwiches.
5. Divide it between two baskets of the air fryer.
6. Turn on the air fry mode for zone 1 basket at 350 degrees f, for 10 minutes.
7. Use the match button for the second zone.
8. Once it's done, serve.

Nutrition:

- (Per serving) calories 617| fat 38 g| sodium 1213mg | carbs40.8 g | fiber 5g| sugar 5.6g | protein 29.5g

Lemony Endive In Curried Yoghurt

Servings: 6
Cooking Time: 10 Minutes

Ingredients:

- 6 heads endive
- 120 ml plain and fat-free yoghurt
- 3 tablespoons lemon juice
- 1 teaspoon garlic powder
- ½ teaspoon curry powder
- Salt and ground black pepper, to taste

Directions:

1. Wash the endives and slice them in half lengthwise.
2. In a bowl, mix together the yoghurt, lemon juice, garlic powder, curry powder, salt and pepper.
3. Brush the endive halves with the marinade, coating them completely. Allow to sit for at least 30 minutes or up to 24 hours.
4. Preheat the air fryer to 160°C.
5. Put the endives in the two air fryer baskets and air fry for 10 minutes.
6. Serve hot.

Cheddar Quiche

Servings:2
Cooking Time:12

Ingredients:

- 4 eggs, organic
- 1-1/4 cup heavy cream
- Salt, pinch
- ½ cup broccoli florets
- ½ cup cheddar cheese, shredded and for sprinkling

Directions:

1. Take a Pyrex pitcher and crack two eggs in it.
2. And fill it with heavy cream, about half the way up.
3. Add in the salt and then add in the broccoli and pour this into two quiche dishes, and top it with shredded cheddar cheese.
4. Now divide it between both zones of baskets.
5. For zone 1, set the time to 10-12 minutes at 325 degrees F.
6. Select the MATCH button for the zone 2 basket.
7. Once done, serve hot.

Nutrition:

- (Per serving) Calories 454| Fat40g | Sodium 406mg | Carbs 4.2g | Fiber 0.6g| Sugar1.3 g | Protein 20g

Jalapeño Popper Dip With Tortilla Chips

Servings:6

Cooking Time: 15 Minutes

Ingredients:

- FOR THE DIP
- 8 ounces cream cheese, at room temperature
- ½ cup sour cream
- 1 cup shredded Cheddar cheese
- ¼ cup shredded Parmesan cheese
- ¼ cup roughly chopped pickled jalapeños
- ½ teaspoon kosher salt
- ½ cup panko bread crumbs
- 2 tablespoons olive oil
- ½ teaspoon dried parsley
- FOR THE TORTILLA CHIPS
- 10 corn tortillas
- 2 tablespoons fresh lime juice
- 1 tablespoon olive oil
- ½ teaspoon kosher salt

Directions:

1. To prep the dip: In a medium bowl, mix the cream cheese, sour cream, Cheddar, Parmesan, jalapeños, and salt until smooth.
2. In a small bowl, combine the panko, olive oil, and parsley.
3. Pour the dip into a 14-ounce ramekin and top with the panko mixture.
4. To prep the chips: Brush both sides of each tortilla with lime juice, then with oil. Sprinkle with the salt. Using a sharp knife or a pizza cutter, cut each tortilla into 4 wedges.
5. To cook the dip and chips: Install a crisper plate in each of the two baskets. Place the ramekin of dip in the Zone 1 basket and insert the basket in the unit. Layer the tortillas in the Zone 2 basket and insert the basket in the unit.
6. Select Zone 1, select BAKE, set the temperature to 350°F, and set the time to 15 minutes.
7. Select Zone 2, select AIR FRY, set the temperature to 375°F, and set the time to 5 minutes. Select SMART FINISH.
8. Press START/PAUSE to begin cooking.
9. When the Zone 2 timer reads 3 minutes, press START/PAUSE. Remove the basket from the unit and give the basket a good shake to redistribute the chips. Reinsert the basket and press START/PAUSE to resume cooking.
10. When cooking is complete, the dip will be bubbling and golden brown and the chips will be crispy. Serve warm.

Nutrition:

- (Per serving) Calories: 406; Total fat: 31g; Saturated fat: 14g; Carbohydrates: 22g; Fiber: 1g; Protein: 11g; Sodium: 539mg

Beefy Swiss Pastry

Servings: 4

Cooking Time: 10 Minutes

Ingredients:

- 455g of beef mince
- 70g sliced fresh mushrooms
- 80g chopped onion
- 1-½ teaspoons minced garlic
- ¾ teaspoon dried rosemary, crushed
- ¾ teaspoon paprika
- ½ teaspoon salt
- ¼ teaspoon pepper
- 1 sheet frozen puff pastry, thawed
- 151g refrigerated mashed potatoes
- 100g shredded Swiss cheese
- 1 large egg
- 2 tablespoons water

Directions:

1. Cook the beef, mushrooms, and onion in a large frying pan over medium heat until the meat is no longer pink and the veggies are cooked, 8-10 minutes| crumble the meat.
2. Cook for a further minute after adding the garlic. Drain. Season with salt and pepper. Remove the pan from the heat and set it aside.
3. Roll puff pastry into a rectangle on a lightly floured surface. Make four little rectangles out of the dough.
4. Over each square, spread around 2 teaspoons of potatoes. ¾ cup beef mixture on top of each| 25g cheese on each.
5. In a small bowl, whisk together the egg and water| brush the wash over the pastry edges.
6. Bring opposing pastry corners over each bundle and pinch seams together to seal. Brush with the rest of the egg mixture.
7. Press either "Zone 1" or "Zone 2" and then rotate the knob to select "Air Fry".
8. Set the temperature to 190 degrees C, and then set the time for 5 minutes to preheat.
9. After preheating, spray the Air-Fryer basket with cooking spray and line with parchment paper. Arrange pastry in a single layer and spritz them with cooking spray.
10. Slide the basket into the Air Fryer and set the time for 10 minutes.
11. After that, turn them and again cook for 3 minutes longer.
12. After cooking time is completed, transfer them onto serving plates and serve.

Beef Jerky Pineapple Jerky

Servings:8

Cooking Time: 6 To 12 Hours

Ingredients:

- FOR THE BEEF JERKY
- ½ cup reduced-sodium soy sauce
- ¼ cup pineapple juice
- 1 tablespoon dark brown sugar
- 1 tablespoon Worcestershire sauce
- ½ teaspoon smoked paprika
- ¼ teaspoon freshly ground black pepper
- ¼ teaspoon red pepper flakes
- 1 pound beef bottom round, trimmed of excess fat, cut into ¼-inch-thick slices
- FOR THE PINEAPPLE JERKY
- 1 pound pineapple, cut into ⅛-inch-thick rounds, pat dry
- 1 teaspoon chili powder (optional)

Directions:

1. To prep the beef jerky: In a large zip-top bag, combine the soy sauce, pineapple juice, brown sugar, Worcestershire sauce, smoked paprika, black pepper, and red pepper flakes.
2. Add the beef slices, seal the bag, and toss to coat the meat in the marinade. Refrigerate overnight or for at least 8 hours.
3. Remove the beef slices and discard the marinade. Using a paper towel, pat the slices dry to remove excess marinade.
4. To prep the pineapple jerky: Sprinkle the pineapple with chili powder (if using).
5. To dehydrate the jerky: Arrange half of the beef slices in a single layer in the Zone 1 basket, making sure they do not overlap. Place a crisper plate on top of the beef slices and arrange the remaining slices in a single layer on top of the crisper plate. Insert the basket in the unit.
6. Repeat this process with the pineapple in the Zone 2 basket and insert the basket in the unit.
7. Select Zone 1, select DEHYDRATE, set the temperature to 150°F, and set the time to 8 hours.
8. Select Zone 2, select DEHYDRATE, set the temperature to 135°F, and set the time to 12 hours.
9. Press START/PAUSE to begin cooking.
10. When the Zone 1 timer reads 2 hours, press START/PAUSE. Remove the basket and check the beef jerky for doneness. If necessary, reinsert the basket and press START/PAUSE to resume cooking.

Nutrition:

- (Per serving) Calories: 171; Total fat: 6.5g; Saturated fat: 2g; Carbohydrates: 2g; Fiber: 0g; Protein: 25g; Sodium: 369mg

Cheese Corn Fritters

Servings: 6
Cooking Time: 15 Minutes

Ingredients:

- 1 egg
- 164g corn
- 2 green onions, diced
- 45g flour
- 29g breadcrumbs
- 117g cheddar cheese, shredded
- ½ tsp onion powder
- ½ tsp garlic powder
- 15g sour cream
- Pepper
- Salt

Directions:

1. In a large bowl, add all ingredients and mix until well combined.
2. Insert a crisper plate in the Tower air fryer baskets.
3. Make patties from the mixture and place them in both baskets.
4. Select zone 1, then select "air fry" mode and set the temperature to 370 degrees F for 12 minutes. Press "match" to match zone 2 settings to zone 1. Press "start/stop" to begin. Turn halfway through.

Crispy Plantain Chips

Servings: 4
Cooking Time: 20 Minutes.

Ingredients:

- 1 green plantain
- 1 teaspoon canola oil
- ½ teaspoon sea salt

Directions:

1. Peel and cut the plantains into long strips using a mandolin slicer.
2. Grease the crisper plates with ½ teaspoon of canola oil.
3. Toss the plantains with salt and remaining canola oil.
4. Divide these plantains in the two crisper plates.
5. Return the crisper plate to the Tower Dual Zone Air Fryer.
6. Choose the Air Fry mode for Zone 1 and set the temperature to 350 degrees F and the time to 20 minutes.
7. Select the "MATCH" button to copy the settings for Zone 2.
8. Initiate cooking by pressing the START/STOP button.
9. Toss the plantains after 10 minutes and resume cooking.
10. Serve warm.

Nutrition:

- (Per serving) Calories 122 | Fat 1.8g |Sodium 794mg | Carbs 17g | Fiber 8.9g | Sugar 1.6g | Protein 14.9g

Bacon-wrapped Dates Bacon-wrapped Scallops

Servings:6
Cooking Time: 12 Minutes

Ingredients:

- FOR THE SCALLOPS
- 6 slices bacon, halved crosswise
- 12 large sea scallops, patted dry
- FOR THE DATES
- 4 slices bacon, cut into thirds
- 12 pitted dates

Directions:

1. To prep the dates: Wrap each piece of bacon around a date and secure with a toothpick.
2. To cook the dates and the bacon for the scallops: Install a crisper plate in each of the two baskets. Place the bacon for the scallops in the Zone 1 basket in a single layer and insert the basket in the unit. Place the bacon-wrapped dates in the Zone 2 basket in a single layer and insert the basket in the unit.
3. Select Zone 1, select AIR FRY, set the temperature to 400°F, and set the time to 12 minutes.
4. Select Zone 2, select AIR FRY, set the temperature to 360°F, and set the time to 10 minutes. Select SMART FINISH.
5. Press START/PAUSE to begin cooking.
6. When the Zone 1 timer reads 9 minutes, press START/PAUSE. Remove the basket from the unit. Wrap each piece of bacon around a scallop and secure with a toothpick. Place the bacon-wrapped scallops in the basket. Reinsert the basket and press START/PAUSE to resume cooking.
7. When the Zone 1 timer reads 4 minutes, press START/PAUSE. Remove the basket and use silicone-tipped tongs to flip the scallops. Reinsert the basket and press START/PAUSE to resume cooking.
8. When cooking is complete, the scallops will be opaque and the bacon around both the scallops and dates will be crisp. Arrange the bacon-wrapped scallops and dates on a serving platter. Serve warm.

Nutrition:

- (Per serving) Calories: 191; Total fat: 2.5g; Saturated fat: 1g; Carbohydrates: 39g; Fiber: 4g; Protein: 3g; Sodium: 115mg

Mozzarella Balls

Servings: 6
Cooking Time: 15 Minutes

Ingredients:

- 2 cups mozzarella, shredded
- 3 tablespoons cornstarch
- 3 tablespoons water
- 2 eggs, beaten
- 1 cup Italian seasoned breadcrumbs
- 1 tablespoon Italian seasoning
- 1½ teaspoons garlic powder
- 1 teaspoon salt
- 1½ teaspoons Parmesan

Directions:

1. Mix mozzarella with parmesan, water and cornstarch in a bowl.
2. Make 1-inch balls out of this mixture.
3. Mix breadcrumbs with seasoning, salt, and garlic powder in a bowl.
4. Dip the balls into the beaten eggs and coat with the breadcrumbs.
5. Place the coated balls in the air fryer baskets.
6. Return the air fryer basket 1 to Zone 1, and basket 2 to Zone 2 of the Tower 2-Basket Air Fryer.
7. Choose the "Air Fry" mode for Zone 1 and set the temperature to 360 degrees F and 13 minutes of cooking time.
8. Select the "MATCH COOK" option to copy the settings for Zone 2.
9. Initiate cooking by pressing the START/PAUSE BUTTON.
10. Toss the balls once cooked halfway through.
11. Serve.

Tater Tots

Servings: 4
Cooking Time: 8 Minutes

Ingredients:

- 16 ounces tater tots
- ½ cup shredded cheddar cheese
- 1½ teaspoons bacon bits
- 2 green onions, chopped
- Sour cream (optional)

Directions:

1. Place a crisper plate in each drawer. Put the tater tots into the drawers in a single layer. Insert the drawers into the unit.
2. Select zone 1, then AIR FRY, then set the temperature to 360 degrees F/ 180 degrees C with a 6-minute timer. To match zone 2 settings to zone 1, choose MATCH. To begin, select START/STOP.
3. When the cooking time is over, add the shredded cheddar cheese, bacon bits, and green onions over the tater tots. Select zone 1, AIR FRY, 360 degrees F/ 180 degrees C, for 4 minutes. Select MATCH. Press START/STOP.
4. Drizzle sour cream over the top before serving.
5. Enjoy!

Nutrition:

- (Per serving) Calories 335 | Fat 19.1g | Sodium 761mg | Carbs 34.1g | Fiber 3g | Sugar 0.6g | Protein 8.9g

Five-ingredient Falafel With Garlic-yoghurt Sauce

Servings: 4
Cooking Time: 15 Minutes

Ingredients:

- Falafel:
- 1 (425 g) can chickpeas, drained and rinsed
- 120 ml fresh parsley
- 2 garlic cloves, minced
- ½ tablespoon ground cumin
- 1 tablespoon wholemeal flour
- Salt
- Garlic-Yoghurt Sauce:
- 240 ml non-fat plain Greek yoghurt
- 1 garlic clove, minced
- 1 tablespoon chopped fresh dill
- 2 tablespoons lemon juice

Directions:

1. Make the Falafel: Preheat the air fryer to 180°C. 2. Put the chickpeas into a food processor. Pulse until mostly chopped, then add the parsley, garlic, and cumin and pulse for another 1 to 2 minutes, or until the ingredients are combined and turning into a dough. 3. Add the flour. Pulse a few more times until combined. The dough will have texture, but the chickpeas should be pulsed into small bits. 4. Using clean hands, roll the dough into 8 balls of equal size, then pat the balls down a bit so they are about ½-thick disks. 5. Spray the zone 1 air fryer basket with olive oil cooking spray, then place the falafel patties in the basket in a single layer, making sure they don't touch each other. 6. Fry in the air fryer for 15 minutes. Make the garlic-yoghurt sauce 7. In a small bowl, combine the yoghurt, garlic, dill, and lemon juice. 8. Once the falafel is done cooking and nicely browned on all sides, remove them from the air fryer and season with salt. 9. Serve hot with a side of dipping sauce.

Taco-spiced Chickpeas And Black Bean Corn Dip

Servings: 7
Cooking Time: 17 Minutes

Ingredients:

- Taco-Spiced Chickpeas:
- Oil, for spraying
- 1 (439 g) can chickpeas, drained
- 1 teaspoon chilli powder
- ½ teaspoon ground cumin
- ½ teaspoon salt
- ½ teaspoon granulated garlic
- 2 teaspoons lime juice
- Black Bean Corn Dip:
- ½ (425 g) can black beans, drained and rinsed
- ½ (425 g) can corn, drained and rinsed
- 60 ml chunky salsa
- 57 g low-fat soft white cheese
- 60 ml shredded low-fat Cheddar cheese
- ½ teaspoon ground cumin
- ½ teaspoon paprika
- Salt and freshly ground black pepper, to taste

Directions:

1. Make the Taco-Spiced Chickpeas :
2. Line the zone 1 air fryer basket with parchment and spray lightly with oil. Place the chickpeas in the prepared basket.
3. Air fry at 200°C for 17 minutes, shaking or stirring the chickpeas and spraying lightly with oil every 5 to 7 minutes.
4. In a small bowl, mix together the chilli powder, cumin, salt, and garlic.
5. When 2 to 3 minutes of cooking time remain, sprinkle half of the seasoning mix over the chickpeas. Finish cooking.
6. Transfer the chickpeas to a medium bowl and toss with the remaining seasoning mix and the lime juice. Serve immediately.
7. Make the Black Bean Corn Dip :
8. Preheat the air fryer to 165°C.
9. In a medium bowl, mix together the black beans, corn, salsa, soft white cheese, Cheddar cheese, cumin, and paprika. Season with salt and pepper and stir until well combined.
10. Spoon the mixture into a baking dish.
11. Place baking dish in the zone 2 air fryer basket and bake until heated through, about 10 minutes.
12. Serve hot.

Cauliflower Gnocchi

Servings: 5
Cooking Time: 17 Minutes.

Ingredients:

- 1 bag frozen cauliflower gnocchi
- 1 ½ tablespoons olive oil
- 1 teaspoon garlic powder
- 3 tablespoons parmesan, grated
- ½ teaspoon dried basil
- Salt to taste
- Fresh chopped parsley for topping

Directions:

1. Toss gnocchi with olive oil, garlic powder, 1 tablespoon of parmesan, salt, and basil in a bowl.
2. Divide the gnocchi in the two crisper plate.
3. Return the crisper plate to the Tower Dual Zone Air Fryer.
4. Choose the Air Fry mode for Zone 1 and set the temperature to 400 degrees F and the time to 10 minutes.
5. Select the "MATCH" button to copy the settings for Zone 2.
6. Initiate cooking by pressing the START/STOP button.
7. Toss the gnocchi once cooked halfway through, then resume cooking.
8. Drizzle the remaining parmesan on top of the gnocchi and cook again for 7 minutes.
9. Serve warm.

Nutrition:

- (Per serving) Calories 134 | Fat 5.9g |Sodium 343mg | Carbs 9.5g | Fiber 0.5g | Sugar 1.1g | Protein 10.4g

Potato Chips

Servings: 4
Cooking Time: 15 Minutes

Ingredients:

- 2 large potatoes, peeled and sliced
- 1½ teaspoons salt
- 1½ teaspoons black pepper
- Oil for misting

Directions:

1. Soak potatoes in cold water for 30 minutes then drain.
2. Pat dry the potato slices and toss them with cracked pepper, salt and oil mist.
3. Spread the potatoes in the air fryer basket.
4. Return the air fryer basket 1 to Zone 1, and basket 2 to Zone 2 of the Tower 2-Basket Air Fryer.
5. Choose the "Air Fry" mode for Zone 1 at 300 degrees F and 16 minutes of cooking time.
6. Select the "MATCH COOK" option to copy the settings for Zone 2.
7. Initiate cooking by pressing the START/PAUSE BUTTON.
8. Toss the fries once cooked halfway through.
9. Serve warm.

Tangy Fried Pickle Spears

Servings: 6
Cooking Time: 15 Minutes

Ingredients:

- 2 jars sweet and sour pickle spears, patted dry
- 2 medium-sized eggs
- 80 ml milk
- 1 teaspoon garlic powder
- 1 teaspoon sea salt
- ½ teaspoon shallot powder
- ⅓ teaspoon chilli powder
- 80 ml plain flour
- Cooking spray

Directions:

1. Preheat the air fryer to 195°C. Spritz the zone 1 air fryer basket with cooking spray.
2. In a bowl, beat together the eggs with milk. In another bowl, combine garlic powder, sea salt, shallot powder, chilli powder and plain flour until well blended.
3. One by one, roll the pickle spears in the powder mixture, then dredge them in the egg mixture. Dip them in the powder mixture a second time for additional coating.
4. Arrange the coated pickles in the prepared basket. Air fry for 15 minutes until golden and crispy, shaking the basket halfway through to ensure even cooking.
5. Transfer to a plate and let cool for 5 minutes before serving.

Fried Pickles

Servings: 4
Cooking Time: 15 Minutes

Ingredients:

- 2 cups sliced dill pickles
- 1 cup flour
- 1 tablespoon garlic powder
- 1 tablespoon Cajun spice
- ½ tablespoon cayenne pepper
- Olive Oil or cooking spray

Directions:

1. Mix together the flour and spices in a bowl.
2. Coat the sliced pickles with the flour mixture.
3. Place a crisper plate in each drawer. Put the pickles in a single layer in each drawer. Insert the drawers into the unit.
4. Select zone 1, then AIR FRY, then set the temperature to 400 degrees F/ 200 degrees C with a 15-minute timer. To match zone 2 settings to zone 1, choose MATCH. To begin, select START/STOP.

Nutrition:

- (Per serving) Calories 161 | Fat 4.1g | Sodium 975mg | Carbs 27.5g | Fiber 2.2g | Sugar 1.5g | Protein 4g

Vegetables And Sides Recipes

Garlic-herb Fried Squash

Servings: 4
Cooking Time: 15 Minutes
Ingredients:

- 5 cups halved small pattypan squash (about 1¼ pounds)
- 1 tablespoon olive oil
- 2 garlic cloves, minced
- ½ teaspoon salt
- ¼ teaspoon dried oregano
- ¼ teaspoon dried thyme
- ¼ teaspoon pepper
- 1 tablespoon minced fresh parsley, for serving

Directions:

1. Place the squash in a large bowl.
2. Mix the oil, garlic, salt, oregano, thyme, and pepper| drizzle over the squash. Toss to coat.
3. Place a crisper plate in both drawers. Put the squash in a single layer in each drawer. Insert the drawers into the unit.
4. Select zone 1, then AIR FRY, then set the temperature to 360 degrees F/ 180 degrees C with a 6-minute timer. To match zone 2 settings to zone 1, choose MATCH. To begin, select START/STOP.
5. Remove the squash from the drawers after the timer has finished. Sprinkle with the parsley.

Air-fried Radishes

Servings: 6
Cooking Time: 15 Minutes
Ingredients:

- 1020g radishes, quartered
- 3 tablespoons olive oil
- 1 tablespoon fresh oregano, minced
- ¼ teaspoon salt
- ⅛ teaspoon black pepper

Directions:

1. Toss radishes with oil, black pepper, salt and oregano in a bowl.
2. Divide the radishes into the Tower 2 Baskets Air Fryer baskets.
3. Return the air fryer basket 1 to Zone 1, and basket 2 to Zone 2 of the Tower 2-Basket Air Fryer.
4. Choose the "Air Fry" mode for Zone 1 at 375 degrees F and 15 minutes of cooking time.
5. Select the "MATCH COOK" option to copy the settings for Zone 2.
6. Initiate cooking by pressing the START/PAUSE BUTTON.
7. Toss the radishes once cooked halfway through.
8. Serve.

Nutrition:

- (Per serving) Calories 270 | Fat 14.6g |Sodium 394mg | Carbs 31.3g | Fiber 7.5g | Sugar 9.7g | Protein 6.4g

Fried Avocado Tacos

Servings: 4

Cooking Time: 10 Minutes

Ingredients:

- For the sauce:
- 2 cups shredded fresh kale or coleslaw mix
- ¼ cup minced fresh cilantro
- ¼ cup plain Greek yogurt
- 2 tablespoons lime juice
- 1 teaspoon honey
- ¼ teaspoon salt
- ¼ teaspoon ground chipotle pepper
- ¼ teaspoon pepper
- For the tacos:
- 1 large egg, beaten
- ¼ cup cornmeal
- ½ teaspoon salt
- ½ teaspoon garlic powder
- ½ teaspoon ground chipotle pepper
- 2 medium avocados, peeled and sliced
- Cooking spray
- 8 flour tortillas or corn tortillas (6 inches), heated up
- 1 medium tomato, chopped
- Crumbled queso fresco (optional)

Directions:

1. Combine the first 8 ingredients in a bowl. Cover and refrigerate until serving.
2. Place the egg in a shallow bowl. In another shallow bowl, mix the cornmeal, salt, garlic powder, and chipotle pepper.
3. Dip the avocado slices in the egg, then into the cornmeal mixture, gently patting to help adhere.
4. Place a crisper plate in both drawers. Put the avocado slices in the drawers in a single layer. Insert the drawers into the unit.
5. Select zone 1, then AIR FRY, then set the temperature to 360 degrees F/ 180 degrees C with a 6-minute timer. To match zone 2 settings to zone 1, choose MATCH. To begin, select START/STOP.
6. Put the avocado slices, prepared sauce, tomato, and queso fresco in the tortillas and serve.

Stuffed Tomatoes

Servings: 2
Cooking Time: 8 Minutes

Ingredients:

- 2 cups brown rice, cooked
- 1 cup tofu, grilled and chopped
- 4 large red tomatoes
- 4 tablespoons basil, chopped
- ¼ tablespoon olive oil
- Salt and black pepper, to taste
- 2 tablespoons lemon juice
- 1 teaspoon red chili powder
- ½ cup Parmesan cheese

Directions:

1. Take a large bowl and mix rice, tofu, basil, olive oil, salt, black pepper, lemon juice, and chili powder.
2. Core the center of the tomatoes.
3. Fill the cavity with the rice mixture.
4. Top them off with the cheese sprinkle.
5. Divide the tomatoes into two air fryer baskets.
6. Turn zone 1 to AIR FRY mode for 8 minutes at 400 degrees F/ 200 degrees C.
7. Select the MATCH button for zone 2.
8. Serve and enjoy.

Saucy Carrots

Servings: 6
Cooking Time: 25 Minutes

Ingredients:

- 1 lb. cup carrots, cut into chunks
- 1 tablespoon sesame oil
- ½ tablespoon ginger, minced
- ½ tablespoon soy sauce
- ½ teaspoon garlic, minced
- ½ tablespoon scallions, chopped, for garnish
- ½ teaspoon sesame seeds for garnish

Directions:

1. Toss all the ginger carrots ingredients, except the sesame seeds and scallions, in a suitable bowl.
2. Divide the carrots in the two crisper plates in a single layer.
3. Return the crisper plates to the Tower Dual Zone Air Fryer.
4. Choose the Air Fry mode for Zone 1 and set the temperature to 390 degrees F/ 200 degrees C and the time to 25 minutes.
5. Select the "MATCH" button to copy the settings for Zone 2.
6. Initiate cooking by pressing the START/STOP button.
7. Toss the carrots once cooked halfway through.
8. Garnish with sesame seeds and scallions.
9. Serve warm.

Breaded Summer Squash

Servings: 4
Cooking Time: 10 Minutes
Ingredients:

- 4 cups yellow summer squash, sliced
- 3 tablespoons olive oil
- ½ teaspoon salt
- ½ teaspoon pepper
- ⅛ teaspoon cayenne pepper
- ¾ cup panko bread crumbs
- ¾ cup grated Parmesan cheese

Directions:

1. Mix crumbs, cheese, cayenne pepper, black pepper, salt and oil in a bowl.
2. Coat the squash slices with the breadcrumb mixture.
3. Place these slices in the air fryer baskets.
4. Return the air fryer basket 1 to Zone 1, and basket 2 to Zone 2 of the Tower 2-Basket Air Fryer.
5. Choose the "Air Fry" mode for Zone 1 at 350 degrees F and 10 minutes of cooking time.
6. Select the "MATCH COOK" option to copy the settings for Zone 2.
7. Initiate cooking by pressing the START/PAUSE BUTTON.
8. Flip the squash slices once cooked half way through.
9. Serve warm.

Nutrition:

- (Per serving) Calories 193 | Fat 1g |Sodium 395mg | Carbs 38.7g | Fiber 1.6g | Sugar 0.9g | Protein 6.6g

Stuffed Sweet Potatoes

Servings: 4
Cooking Time: 55 Minutes
Ingredients:

- 2 medium sweet potatoes
- 1 teaspoon olive oil
- 1 cup cooked chopped spinach, drained
- 1 cup shredded cheddar cheese, divided
- 2 cooked bacon strips, crumbled
- 1 green onion, chopped
- ¼ cup fresh cranberries, coarsely chopped
- ⅓ cup chopped pecans, toasted
- 2 tablespoons butter
- ¼ teaspoon kosher salt
- ¼ teaspoon pepper

Directions:

1. Brush the sweet potatoes with the oil.
2. Place a crisper plate in both drawers. Add one sweet potato to each drawer. Place the drawers in the unit.
3. Select zone 1, then AIR FRY, then set the temperature to 360 degrees F/ 180 degrees C with a 40-minute timer. To match zone 2 settings to zone 1, choose MATCH. To begin, select START/STOP.
4. Remove the sweet potatoes from the drawers after the timer has finished. Cut them in half lengthwise. Scoop out the pulp, leaving a ¼-inch thick shell. 5. Put the pulp in a large bowl and stir in the spinach, ¾ cup of cheese, bacon, onion, pecans, cranberries, butter, salt, and pepper.
5. Spoon the mixture into the potato shells, mounding the mixture slightly.
6. Place a crisper plate in each drawer. Put one filled potato into each drawer and insert them into the unit.
7. Select zone 1, then AIR FRY, then set the temperature to 360 degrees F/ 180 degrees C with a 10-minute timer. To match zone 2 settings to zone 1, choose MATCH. To begin, select START/STOP.
8. Sprinkle with the remaining ¼ cup of cheese. Cook using the same settings until the cheese is melted .

Delicious Potatoes & Carrots

Servings: 8
Cooking Time: 25 Minutes

Ingredients:

- 453g carrots, sliced
- 2 tsp smoked paprika
- 21g sugar
- 30ml olive oil
- 453g potatoes, diced
- 1/4 tsp thyme
- 1/2 tsp dried oregano
- 1 tsp garlic powder
- Pepper
- Salt

Directions:

1. In a bowl, toss carrots and potatoes with 1 tablespoon of oil.
2. Insert a crisper plate in the Tower air fryer baskets.
3. Add carrots and potatoes to both baskets.
4. Select zone 1 then select "air fry" mode and set the temperature to 390 degrees F for 15 minutes. Press "match" to match zone 2 settings to zone 1. Press "start/stop" to begin.
5. In a mixing bowl, add cooked potatoes, carrots, smoked paprika, sugar, oil, thyme, oregano, garlic powder, pepper, and salt and toss well.
6. Return carrot and potato mixture into the air fryer basket and cook for 10 minutes more.

Nutrition:

- (Per serving) Calories 101 | Fat 3.6g |Sodium 62mg | Carbs 16.6g | Fiber 3g | Sugar 5.1g | Protein 1.6g

Kale And Spinach Chips

Servings: 2
Cooking Time: 6 Minutes

Ingredients:

- 2 cups spinach, torn in pieces and stem removed
- 2 cups kale, torn in pieces, stems removed
- 1 tablespoon olive oil
- Sea salt, to taste
- 1/3 cup Parmesan cheese

Directions:

1. Take a bowl and add spinach to it.
2. Take another bowl and add kale to it.
3. Season both of them with olive oil and sea salt.
4. Add the kale to the zone 1 basket and spinach to the zone 2 basket.
5. Select AIR FRY mode for zone 1 at 350 degrees F/ 175 degrees C for 6 minutes.
6. Set zone 2 to AIR FRY mode at 350 degrees F/ 175 degrees C for 5 minutes.
7. Once done, take out the crispy chips and sprinkle Parmesan cheese on top. 8. Serve and Enjoy.

Zucchini With Stuffing

Servings:3
Cooking Time:20

Ingredients:

- 1 cup quinoa, rinsed
- 1 cup black olives
- 6 medium zucchinis, about 2 pounds
- 2 cups cannellini beans, drained
- 1 white onion, chopped
- ¼ cup almonds, chopped
- 4 cloves of garlic, chopped
- 4 tablespoons olive oil
- 1 cup of water
- 2 cups Parmesan cheese, for topping

Directions:

1. First wash the zucchini and cut it lengthwise.
2. Take a skillet and heat oil in it
3. Sauté the onion in olive oil for a few minutes.
4. Then add the quinoa and water and let it cook for 8 minutes with the lid on the top.
5. Transfer the quinoa to a bowl and add all remaining ingredients excluding zucchini and Parmesan cheese.
6. Scoop out the seeds of zucchinis.
7. Fill the cavity of zucchinis with bowl mixture.
8. Top it with a handful of Parmesan cheese.
9. Arrange 4 zucchinis in both air fryer baskets.
10. Select zone1 basket at AIR FRY for 20 minutes and adjusting the temperature to 390 degrees F.
11. Use the Match button to select the same setting for zone 2.
12. Serve and enjoy.

Nutrition:

- (Per serving) Calories 1171| Fat 48.6g| Sodium 1747mg | Carbs 132.4g | Fiber 42.1g | Sugar 11.5g | Protein 65.7g

Brussels Sprouts

Servings: 2
Cooking Time: 20 Minutes

Ingredients:

- 2 pounds Brussels sprouts
- 2 tablespoons avocado oil
- Salt and pepper, to taste
- 1 cup pine nuts, roasted

Directions:

1. Trim the bottom of the Brussels sprouts.
2. Take a bowl and combine the avocado oil, salt, and black pepper.
3. Toss the Brussels sprouts into the bowl and mix well.
4. Divide the mixture into both air fryer baskets.
5. For zone 1 set to AIR FRY mode for 20 minutes at 390 degrees F/ 200 degrees C.
6. Select the MATCH button for the zone 2 basket.
7. Once the Brussels sprouts get crisp and tender, take out and serve.

Flavourful Mexican Cauliflower

Servings: 4
Cooking Time: 12 Minutes

Ingredients:

- 1 medium cauliflower head, cut into florets
- ½ tsp turmeric
- 1 tsp onion powder
- 2 tsp garlic powder
- 2 tsp parsley
- 1 lime juice
- 30ml olive oil
- 1 tsp chilli powder
- 1 tsp cumin
- Pepper
- Salt

Directions:

1. In a bowl, toss cauliflower florets with onion powder, garlic powder, parsley, oil, chilli powder, turmeric, cumin, pepper, and salt.
2. Insert a crisper plate in the Tower air fryer baskets.
3. Add cauliflower florets in both baskets.
4. Select zone 1, then select "air fry" mode and set the temperature to 390 degrees F for 12 minutes. Press "match" to match zone 2 settings to zone 1. Press "start/stop" to begin. Stir halfway through.
5. Drizzle lime juice over cauliflower florets.

Nutrition:

- (Per serving) Calories 108 | Fat 7.4g |Sodium 91mg | Carbs 10g | Fiber 4.1g | Sugar 4.1g | Protein 3.4g

Fried Asparagus

Servings: 4
Cooking Time: 6 Minutes

Ingredients:

- ¼ cup mayonnaise
- 4 teaspoons olive oil
- 1½ teaspoons grated lemon zest
- 1 garlic clove, minced
- ½ teaspoon pepper
- ¼ teaspoon seasoned salt
- 1-pound fresh asparagus, trimmed
- 2 tablespoons shredded parmesan cheese
- Lemon wedges (optional)

Directions:

1. In a large bowl, combine the first 6 ingredients.
2. Add the asparagus| toss to coat.
3. Put a crisper plate in both drawers. Put the asparagus in a single layer in each drawer. Top with the parmesan cheese. Place the drawers into the unit.
4. Select zone 1, then AIR FRY, then set the temperature to 375 degrees F/ 190 degrees C with a 6-minute timer. To match zone 2 settings to zone 1, choose MATCH. To begin, select START/STOP.
5. Remove the asparagus from the drawers after the timer has finished.

Caprese Panini With Zucchini Chips

Servings:4
Cooking Time: 20 Minutes

Ingredients:

- FOR THE PANINI
- 4 tablespoons pesto
- 8 slices Italian-style sandwich bread
- 1 tomato, diced
- 6 ounces fresh mozzarella cheese, shredded
- ¼ cup mayonnaise
- FOR THE ZUCCHINI CHIPS
- ½ cup all-purpose flour
- 2 large eggs
- ¼ teaspoon freshly ground black pepper
- ⅛ teaspoon kosher salt
- ½ cup panko bread crumbs
- ¼ cup grated Parmesan cheese
- 1 teaspoon Italian seasoning
- 1 medium zucchini, cut into ¼-inch-thick rounds
- 2 tablespoons vegetable oil

Directions:

1. To prep the panini: Spread 1 tablespoon of pesto each on 4 slices of the bread. Layer the diced tomato and shredded mozzarella on the other 4 slices of bread. Top the tomato/cheese mixture with the pesto-coated bread, pesto-side down, to form 4 sandwiches.
2. Spread the outside of each sandwich (both bread slices) with a thin layer of the mayonnaise.
3. To prep the zucchini chips: Set up a breading station with three small shallow bowls. Place the flour in the first bowl. In the second bowl, beat together the eggs, salt, and black pepper. Place the panko, Parmesan, and Italian seasoning in the third bowl.
4. Bread the zucchini in this order: First, dip the slices into the flour, coating both sides. Then, dip into the beaten egg. Finally, coat in the panko mixture. Drizzle the zucchini on both sides with the oil.
5. To cook the panini and zucchini chips: Install a crisper plate in each of the two baskets. Place 2 sandwiches in the Zone 1 basket and insert the basket in the unit. Place half of the zucchini chips in a single layer in the Zone 2 basket and insert the basket in the unit.
6. Select Zone 1, select AIR FRY, set the temperature to 375°F, and set the timer to 20 minutes.
7. Select Zone 2, select AIR FRY, set the temperature to 400°F, and set the timer to 20 minutes. Select SMART FINISH.
8. Press START/PAUSE to begin cooking.
9. When the Zone 1 timer reads 15 minutes, press START/PAUSE. Remove the basket, and use silicone-tipped tongs or a spatula to flip the sandwiches. Reinsert the basket and press START/PAUSE to resume cooking.
10. When both timers read 10 minutes, press START/PAUSE. Remove the Zone 1 basket and transfer the sandwiches to a plate. Place the remaining 2 sandwiches into the basket and insert the basket in the unit. Remove the Zone 2 basket and transfer the zucchini chips to a serving plate. Place the remaining zucchini chips in the basket. Reinsert the basket and press START/PAUSE to resume cooking.
11. When the Zone 1 timer reads 5 minutes, press START/PAUSE. Remove the basket and flip the sandwiches. Reinsert the basket and press START/PAUSE to resume cooking.
12. When cooking is complete, the panini should be toasted and the zucchini chips golden brown and crisp.
13. Cut each panini in half. Serve hot with zucchini chips on the side.

Nutrition:

- (Per serving) Calories: 751; Total fat: 39g; Saturated fat: 9.5g; Carbohydrates: 77g; Fiber: 3.5g; Protein: 23g; Sodium: 1,086mg

Fried Artichoke Hearts

Servings: 6
Cooking Time: 10 Minutes
Ingredients:

- 3 cans Quartered Artichokes, drained
- ½ cup mayonnaise
- 1 cup panko breadcrumbs
- ⅓ cup grated Parmesan
- salt and black pepper to taste
- Parsley for garnish

Directions:

1. Mix mayonnaise with salt and black pepper and keep the sauce aside.
2. Spread panko breadcrumbs in a bowl.
3. Coat the artichoke pieces with the breadcrumbs.
4. As you coat the artichokes, place them in the two crisper plates in a single layer, then spray them with cooking oil.
5. Return the crisper plates to the Tower Dual Zone Air Fryer.
6. Choose the Air Fry mode for Zone 1 and set the temperature to 375 degrees F/ 190 degrees C and the time to 10 minutes.
7. Select the "MATCH" button to copy the settings for Zone 2.
8. Initiate cooking by pressing the START/STOP button.
9. Flip the artichokes once cooked halfway through, then resume cooking.
10. Serve warm with mayo sauce.

Fish And Seafood Recipes

Bacon Halibut Steak

Servings: 4
Cooking Time: 10 Minutes
Ingredients:

- 680 g halibut steaks (170 g each fillet)
- 1 teaspoon avocado oil
- 1 teaspoon ground black pepper
- 110 g bacon, sliced

Directions:

1. Sprinkle the halibut steaks with avocado oil and ground black pepper.
2. Then wrap the fish in the bacon slices and put in the two air fryer baskets.
3. Cook the fish at 200°C for 5 minutes per side.

Honey Sriracha Mahi Mahi

Servings: 4
Cooking Time: 7 Minutes

Ingredients:

- 3 pounds mahi-mahi
- 6 tablespoons honey
- 4 tablespoons sriracha
- Salt, to taste
- Cooking spray

Directions:

1. In a small bowl, mix the sriracha sauce and honey. Mix well.
2. Season the fish with salt and pour the honey mixture over it. Let it sit at room temperature for 20 minutes.
3. Place a crisper plate in each drawer. Put the fish in a single layer in each. Insert the drawers into the unit.
4. Select zone 1, then AIR FRY, then set the temperature to 400 degrees F/ 200 degrees C with a 7-minute timer. To match zone 2 settings to zone 1, choose MATCH. To begin, select START/STOP.
5. Remove the fish from the drawers after the timer has finished.

Nutrition:

- (Per serving) Calories 581 | Fat 22g | Sodium 495mg | Carbs 26g | Fiber 4g | Sugar 26g | Protein 68g

Keto Baked Salmon With Pesto

Servings:2
Cooking Time:18

Ingredients:

- 4 salmon fillets, 2 inches thick
- 2 ounces green pesto
- Salt and black pepper
- ½ tablespoon of canola oil, for greasing
- 1-1/2 cup mayonnaise
- 2 tablespoons Greek yogurt
- Salt and black pepper, to taste

Directions:

1. Rub the salmon with pesto, salt, oil, and black pepper.
2. In a small bowl, whisk together all the green sauce ingredients.
3. Divide the fish fillets between both the baskets.
4. Set zone 1 to air fry mode for 18 minutes at 390 degrees F.
5. Select MATCH button for Zone 2 basket.
6. Once the cooking is done, serve it with green sauce drizzle.
7. Enjoy.

Nutrition:

- (Per serving) Calories 1165 | Fat80.7 g| Sodium 1087 mg | Carbs 33.1g | Fiber 0.5g | Sugar11.5 g | Protein 80.6g

Steamed Cod With Garlic And Swiss Chard

Servings: 4
Cooking Time: 12 Minutes

Ingredients:

- 1 teaspoon salt
- ½ teaspoon dried oregano
- ½ teaspoon dried thyme
- ½ teaspoon garlic powder
- 4 cod fillets
- ½ white onion, thinly sliced
- 135 g Swiss chard, washed, stemmed, and torn into pieces
- 60 ml olive oil
- 1 lemon, quartered

Directions:

1. Preheat the air fryer to 192°C.
2. In a small bowl, whisk together the salt, oregano, thyme, and garlic powder.
3. Tear off four pieces of aluminum foil, with each sheet being large enough to envelop one cod fillet and a quarter of the vegetables.
4. Place a cod fillet in the middle of each sheet of foil, then sprinkle on all sides with the spice mixture.
5. In each foil packet, place a quarter of the onion slices and 30 g Swiss chard, then drizzle 1 tablespoon olive oil and squeeze ¼ lemon over the contents of each foil packet.
6. Fold and seal the sides of the foil packets and then place them into the two air fryer drawers. Steam for 12 minutes.
7. Remove from the drawers, and carefully open each packet to avoid a steam burn.

Lemon Pepper Fish Fillets

Servings: 4
Cooking Time: 10 Minutes

Ingredients:

- 4 tilapia fillets
- 30ml olive oil
- 2 tbsp lemon zest
- ⅛ tsp paprika
- 1 tsp garlic, minced
- 1 ½ tsp ground peppercorns
- Pepper
- Salt

Directions:

1. In a small bowl, mix oil, peppercorns, paprika, garlic, lemon zest, pepper, and salt.
2. Brush the fish fillets with oil mixture.
3. Insert a crisper plate in the Tower air fryer baskets.
4. Place fish fillets in both baskets.
5. Select zone 1 then select "air fry" mode and set the temperature to 390 degrees F for 10 minutes. Press "match" to match zone 2 settings to zone 1. Press "start/stop" to begin.

Nutrition:

- (Per serving) Calories 203 | Fat 9g |Sodium 99mg | Carbs 0.9g | Fiber 0.2g | Sugar 0.2g | Protein 32.1g

Tilapia Sandwiches With Tartar Sauce

Servings: 4
Cooking Time: 17 Minutes
Ingredients:

- 160 g mayonnaise
- 2 tablespoons dried minced onion
- 1 dill pickle spear, finely chopped
- 2 teaspoons pickle juice
- ¼ teaspoon salt
- ⅛ teaspoon freshly ground black pepper
- 40 g plain flour
- 1 egg, lightly beaten
- 200 g panko bread crumbs
- 2 teaspoons lemon pepper
- 4 (170 g) tilapia fillets
- Olive oil spray
- 4 soft sub rolls
- 4 lettuce leaves

Directions:

1. To make the tartar sauce, in a small bowl, whisk the mayonnaise, dried onion, pickle, pickle juice, salt, and pepper until blended. Refrigerate while you make the fish.
2. Scoop the flour onto a plate; set aside.
3. Put the beaten egg in a medium shallow bowl.
4. On another plate, stir together the panko and lemon pepper.
5. Preheat the air fryer to 205°C.
6. Dredge the tilapia fillets in the flour, in the egg, and press into the panko mixture to coat.
7. Once the unit is preheated, spray the zone 1 basket with olive oil and place a baking paper liner into the basket. Place the prepared fillets on the liner in a single layer. Lightly spray the fillets with olive oil.
8. cook for 8 minutes, remove the basket, carefully flip the fillets, and spray them with more olive oil. Reinsert the basket to resume cooking.
9. When the cooking is complete, the fillets should be golden and crispy and a food thermometer should register 65°C. Place each cooked fillet in a sub roll, top with a little bit of tartar sauce and lettuce, and serve.

Basil Cheese S·saltalmon

Servings: 4
Cooking Time:7 Minutes
Ingredients:

- 4 salmon fillets
- 1/4 cup parmesan cheese, grated
- 5 fresh basil leaves, minced
- 2 tbsp mayonnaise
- 1/2 lemon juice
- Pepper

Directions:

1. Preheat the air fryer to 400 F.
2. Brush salmon fillets with lemon juice and season with pepper and salt.
3. In a small bowl, mix mayonnaise, basil, and cheese.
4. Spray air fryer basket with cooking spray.
5. Place salmon fillets into the air fryer basket and brush with mayonnaise mixture and cook for 7 minutes.
6. Serve and enjoy.

Seafood Shrimp Omelet

Servings:2
Cooking Time:15
Ingredients:

- 6 large shrimp, shells removed and chopped
- 6 eggs, beaten
- ½ tablespoon of butter, melted
- 2 tablespoons green onions, sliced
- 1/3 cup of mushrooms, chopped
- 1 pinch paprika
- Salt and black pepper, to taste
- Oil spray, for greasing

Directions:

1. In a large bowl whisk the eggs and add chopped shrimp, butter, green onions, mushrooms, paprika, salt, and black pepper.
2. Take two cake pans that fit inside the air fryer and grease them with oil spray.
3. Pour the egg mixture between the cake pans and place it in two baskets of the air fryer.
4. Turn on the BAKE function of zone 1, and let it cook for 15 minutes at 320 degrees F.
5. Select the MATCH button to match the cooking time for the zone 2 basket.
6. Once the cooking cycle completes, take out, and serve hot.

Nutrition:

- (Per serving) Calories 300 | Fat 17.5g| Sodium 368mg | Carbs 2.9g | Fiber 0.3g | Sugar1.4 g | Protein32.2 g

Tandoori Prawns

Servings: 4
Cooking Time: 6 Minutes
Ingredients:

- 455 g jumbo raw prawns (21 to 25 count), peeled and deveined
- 1 tablespoon minced fresh ginger
- 3 cloves garlic, minced
- 5 g chopped fresh coriander or parsley, plus more for garnish
- 1 teaspoon ground turmeric
- 1 teaspoon garam masala
- 1 teaspoon smoked paprika
- 1 teaspoon kosher or coarse sea salt
- ½ to 1 teaspoon cayenne pepper
- 2 tablespoons olive oil (for Paleo) or melted ghee
- 2 teaspoons fresh lemon juice

Directions:

1. In a large bowl, combine the prawns, ginger, garlic, coriander, turmeric, garam masala, paprika, salt, and cayenne. Toss well to coat. Add the oil or ghee and toss again. Marinate at room temperature for 15 minutes, or cover and refrigerate for up to 8 hours.
2. Place the prawns in a single layer in the two air fryer baskets. Set the air fryer to 165°C for 6 minutes. Transfer the prawns to a serving platter. Cover and let the prawns finish cooking in the residual heat, about 5 minutes.
3. Sprinkle the prawns with the lemon juice and toss to coat. Garnish with additional cilantro and serve.

Southwestern Fish Fillets

Servings: 4
Cooking Time: 16 Minutes
Ingredients:

- 455g trout fillets
- 1 tsp garlic powder
- 29g breadcrumbs
- 15ml olive oil
- 1 tsp chilli powder
- 1 tsp onion powder

Directions:

1. In a small bowl, mix breadcrumbs, garlic powder, onion powder, and chilli powder.
2. Brush fish fillets with oil and coat with breadcrumbs.
3. Insert a crisper plate in the Tower air fryer baskets.
4. Place coated fish fillets in both baskets.
5. Select zone 1 then select "air fry" mode and set the temperature to 375 degrees F for 16 minutes. Press "match" and "start/stop" to begin.

Nutrition:

- (Per serving) Calories 272 | Fat 13.5g |Sodium 120mg | Carbs 5g | Fiber 0.6g | Sugar 0.7g | Protein 31.1g

Crustless Prawn Quiche

Servings: 2
Cooking Time: 20 Minutes
Ingredients:

- Vegetable oil
- 4 large eggs
- 120 ml single cream
- 110 g raw prawns, chopped
- 120 g shredded Parmesan or Swiss cheese
- 235 g chopped spring onions
- 1 teaspoon sweet smoked paprika
- 1 teaspoon Herbes de Provence
- 1 teaspoon black pepper
- ½ to 1 teaspoon kosher or coarse sea salt

Directions:

1. Generously grease a baking pan with vegetable oil.
2. In a large bowl, beat together the eggs and single cream. Add the prawns, 90 g of the cheese, the scallions, paprika, Herbes de Provence, pepper, and salt. Stir with a fork to thoroughly combine. Pour the egg mixture into the prepared pan.
3. Place the pan in the zone 1 air fryer basket. Set the air fryer to 150°C for 20 minutes. After 17 minutes, sprinkle the remaining 30 g cheese on top and cook for the remaining 3 minutes, or until the cheese has melted, the eggs are set, and a toothpick inserted into the center comes out clean.
4. Serve the quiche warm or at room temperature.

Scallops With Greens

Servings: 8
Cooking Time: 13 Minutes

Ingredients:

- ¾ cup heavy whipping cream
- 1 tablespoon tomato paste
- 1 tablespoon chopped fresh basil
- 1 teaspoon garlic, minced
- ½ teaspoons salt
- ½ teaspoons pepper
- 12 ounces frozen spinach thawed
- 8 jumbo sea scallops
- Vegetable oil to spray

Directions:

1. Season the scallops with vegetable oil, salt, and pepper in a bowl
2. Mix cream with spinach, basil, garlic, salt, pepper, and tomato paste in a bowl.
3. Pour this mixture over the scallops and mix gently.
4. Divide the scallops in the Air Fryers Baskets without using the crisper plate.
5. Return the crisper plate to the Tower Dual Zone Air Fryer.
6. Choose the Air Fry mode for Zone 1 and set the temperature to 390 degrees F and the time to 13 minutes|
7. Select the "MATCH" button to copy the settings for Zone 2.
8. Initiate cooking by pressing the START/STOP button.
9. Serve right away

Roasted Halibut Steaks With Parsley

Servings: 4
Cooking Time: 10 Minutes

Ingredients:

- 455 g halibut steaks
- 60 ml vegetable oil
- 2½ tablespoons Worcester sauce
- 2 tablespoons honey
- 2 tablespoons vermouth or white wine vinegar
- 1 tablespoon freshly squeezed lemon juice
- 1 tablespoon fresh parsley leaves, coarsely chopped
- Salt and pepper, to taste
- 1 teaspoon dried basil

Directions:

1. Preheat the air fryer to 200°C.
2. Put all the ingredients in a large mixing dish and gently stir until the fish is coated evenly.
3. Transfer the fish to the zone 1 air fryer drawer and roast for 10 minutes, flipping the fish halfway through, or until the fish reaches an internal temperature of at least 64°C on a meat thermometer.
4. Let the fish cool for 5 minutes and serve.

Tilapia With Mojo And Crispy Plantains

Servings:4

Cooking Time: 30 Minutes

Ingredients:

- FOR THE TILAPIA
- 4 tilapia fillets (6 ounces each)
- 2 tablespoons all-purpose flour
- Nonstick cooking spray
- ¼ cup freshly squeezed orange juice
- 3 tablespoons fresh lime juice
- 2 tablespoons olive oil
- 1 tablespoon minced garlic
- ½ teaspoon ground cumin
- ¼ teaspoon kosher salt
- FOR THE PLANTAINS
- 1 large green plantain
- 2 cups cold water
- 2 teaspoons kosher salt
- Nonstick cooking spray

Directions:

1. To prep the tilapia: Dust both sides of the tilapia fillets with the flour, then spritz with cooking spray.
2. In a small bowl, whisk together the orange juice, lime juice, oil, garlic, cumin, and salt. Set the mojo sauce aside.
3. To prep the plantains: Cut the ends from the plantain, then remove and discard the peel. Slice the plantain into 1-inch rounds.
4. In a large bowl, combine the water, salt, and plantains. Let soak for 15 minutes.
5. Drain the plantains and pat them dry with paper towels. Spray with cooking spray.
6. To cook the tilapia and plantains: Install a crisper plate in each of the two baskets. Place the tilapia in a single layer in the Zone 1 basket (work in batches if needed) and insert the basket in the unit. Place the plantains in the Zone 2 basket and insert the basket in the unit.
7. Select Zone 1, select AIR FRY, set the temperature to 390°F, and set the timer to 10 minutes.
8. Select Zone 2, select AIR FRY, set the temperature to 390°F, and set the timer to 30 minutes. Select SMART FINISH.
9. Press START/PAUSE to begin cooking.
10. When the Zone 2 timer reads 10 minutes, press START/PAUSE. Remove the basket and use silicone-tipped tongs to transfer the plantains, which should be tender, to a cutting board. Use the bottom of a heavy glass to smash each plantain flat. Spray both sides with cooking spray and place them back in the basket. Reinsert the basket and press START/PAUSE to resume cooking.
11. When the Zone 1 timer reads 5 minutes, press START/PAUSE. Remove the basket. Spoon half of the mojo sauce over the tilapia. Reinsert the basket and press START/PAUSE to resume cooking.
12. When cooking is complete, the fish should be cooked through and the plantains crispy. Serve the tilapia and plantains with the remaining mojo sauce for dipping.

Nutrition:

- (Per serving) Calories: 380; Total fat: 21g; Saturated fat: 2g; Carbohydrates: 20g; Fiber: 1g; Protein: 35g; Sodium: 217mg

Crispy Parmesan Cod

Servings: 2
Cooking Time: 10 Minutes

Ingredients:

- 455g cod filets
- Salt and black pepper, to taste
- ½ cup flour
- 2 large eggs, beaten
- ½ teaspoon salt
- 1 cup Panko
- ½ cup grated parmesan
- 2 teaspoons old bay seasoning
- ½ teaspoon garlic powder
- Olive oil spray

Directions:

1. Rub the cod fillets with black pepper and salt.
2. Mix panko with parmesan cheese, old bay seasoning, and garlic powder in a bowl.
3. Mix flour with salt in another bowl.
4. Dredge the cod filets in the flour then dip in the eggs and coat with the Panko mixture.
5. Place the cod fillets in the air fryer baskets.
6. Return the air fryer basket 1 to Zone 1, and basket 2 to Zone 2 of the Tower 2-Basket Air Fryer.
7. Choose the "Air Fry" mode for Zone 1 and set the temperature to 400 degrees F and 10 minutes of cooking time.
8. Select the "MATCH COOK" option to copy the settings for Zone 2.
9. Initiate cooking by pressing the START/PAUSE BUTTON.
10. Flip the cod fillets once cooked halfway through.
11. Serve warm.

Nutrition:

- (Per serving) Calories 275 | Fat 1.4g |Sodium 582mg | Carbs 31.5g | Fiber 1.1g | Sugar 0.1g | Protein 29.8g

Blackened Red Snapper

Servings: 4
Cooking Time: 8 To 10 Minutes

Ingredients:

- 1½ teaspoons black pepper
- ¼ teaspoon thyme
- ¼ teaspoon garlic powder
- ⅛ teaspoon cayenne pepper
- 1 teaspoon olive oil
- 4 red snapper fillet portions, skin on, 110 g each
- 4 thin slices lemon
- Cooking spray

Directions:

1. Mix the spices and oil together to make a paste. Rub into both sides of the fish.
2. Spray the two air fryer drawers with nonstick cooking spray and lay snapper steaks in drawers, skin-side down.
3. Place a lemon slice on each piece of fish.
4. Roast at 200°C for 8 to 10 minutes. The fish will not flake when done, but it should be white through the center.

South Indian Fried Fish

Servings: 4
Cooking Time: 8 Minutes

Ingredients:

- 2 tablespoons olive oil
- 2 tablespoons fresh lime or lemon juice
- 1 teaspoon minced fresh ginger
- 1 clove garlic, minced
- 1 teaspoon ground turmeric
- ½ teaspoon kosher or coarse sea salt
- ¼ to ½ teaspoon cayenne pepper
- 455 g tilapia fillets (2 to 3 fillets)
- Olive oil spray
- Lime or lemon wedges (optional)

Directions:

1. In a large bowl, combine the oil, lime juice, ginger, garlic, turmeric, salt, and cayenne. Stir until well combined; set aside.
2. Cut each tilapia fillet into three or four equal-size pieces. Add the fish to the bowl and gently mix until all of the fish is coated in the marinade. Marinate for 10 to 15 minutes at room temperature.
3. Spray the air fryer basket with olive oil spray. Place the fish in the basket and spray the fish. Set the air fryer to 165°C for 3 minutes to partially cook the fish. Set the air fryer to 205°C for 5 minutes to finish cooking and crisp up the fish.
4. Carefully remove the fish from the basket. Serve hot, with lemon wedges if desired.

Sweet & Spicy Fish Fillets

Servings: 4
Cooking Time: 8 Minutes

Ingredients:

- 4 salmon fillets
- 1 tsp smoked paprika
- 1 tsp chilli powder
- ½ tsp red pepper flakes, crushed
- ½ tsp garlic powder
- 85g honey
- Pepper
- Salt

Directions:

1. In a small bowl, mix honey, garlic powder, chilli powder, paprika, red pepper flakes, pepper, and salt.
2. Brush fish fillets with honey mixture.
3. Insert a crisper plate in the Tower air fryer baskets.
4. Place fish fillets in both baskets.
5. Select zone 1, then select "air fry" mode and set the temperature to 390 degrees F for 8 minutes. Press "match" and then"start/stop" to begin.

Nutrition:

- (Per serving) Calories 305 | Fat 11.2g |Sodium 125mg | Carbs 18.4g | Fiber 0.6g | Sugar 17.5g | Protein 34.8g

Simple Buttery Cod & Salmon On Bed Of Fennel And Carrot

Servings: 4
Cooking Time: 13 To 14 Minutes
Ingredients:

- Simple Buttery Cod:
- 2 cod fillets, 110 g each
- 2 tablespoons salted butter, melted
- 1 teaspoon Old Bay seasoning
- ½ medium lemon, sliced
- Salmon on Bed of Fennel and Carrot:
- 1 fennel bulb, thinly sliced
- 1 large carrot, peeled and sliced
- 1 small onion, thinly sliced
- 60 ml low-fat sour cream
- ¼ teaspoon coarsely ground pepper
- 2 salmon fillets, 140 g each

Directions:

1. Make the Simple Buttery Cod :
2. Place cod fillets into a round baking dish. Brush each fillet with butter and sprinkle with Old Bay seasoning. Lay two lemon slices on each fillet. Cover the dish with foil and place into the zone 1 air fryer basket.
3. Adjust the temperature to 175°C and bake for 8 minutes. Flip halfway through the cooking time. When cooked, internal temperature should be at least 65°C. Serve warm.
4. Make the Salmon on Bed of Fennel and Carrot :
5. Combine the fennel, carrot, and onion in a bowl and toss.
6. Put the vegetable mixture into a baking pan. Roast in the zone 2 air fryer basket at 205°C for 4 minutes or until the vegetables are crisp-tender.
7. Remove the pan from the air fryer. Stir in the sour cream and sprinkle the vegetables with the pepper.
8. Top with the salmon fillets.
9. Return the pan to the air fryer. Roast for another 9 to 10 minutes or until the salmon just barely flakes when tested with a fork.

Frozen Breaded Fish Fillet

Servings:2
Cooking Time:12
Ingredients:

- 4 Frozen Breaded Fish Fillet
- Oil spray, for greasing
- 1 cup mayonnaise

Directions:

1. Take the frozen fish fillets out of the bag and place them in both baskets of the air fryer.
2. Lightly grease it with oil spray.
3. Set the Zone 1 basket to 380 degrees F fo12 minutes.
4. Select the MATCH button for the zone 2 basket.
5. hit the start button to start cooking.
6. Once the cooking is done, serve the fish hot with mayonnaise.

Nutrition:

- (Per serving) Calories 921| Fat 61.5g| Sodium 1575mg | Carbs 69g | Fiber 2g | Sugar 9.5g | Protein 29.1g

Fried Lobster Tails

Servings: 4
Cooking Time: 18 Minutes

Ingredients:

- 4 (4-oz) lobster tails
- 8 tablespoons butter, melted
- 2 teaspoons lemon zest
- 2 garlic cloves, grated
- Salt and black pepper, ground to taste
- 2 teaspoons fresh parsley, chopped
- 4 wedges lemon

Directions:

1. Spread the lobster tails into Butterfly, slit the top to expose the lobster meat while keeping the tail intact.
2. Place two lobster tails in each of the crisper plate with their lobster meat facing up.
3. Mix melted butter with lemon zest and garlic in a bowl.
4. Brush the butter mixture on top of the lobster tails.
5. And drizzle salt and black pepper on top.
6. Return the crisper plate to the Tower Dual Zone Air Fryer.
7. Choose the Air Fry mode for Zone 1 and set the temperature to 390 degrees F and the time to 18 minutes|
8. Select the "MATCH" button to copy the settings for Zone 2.
9. Initiate cooking by pressing the START/STOP button.
10. Garnish with parsley and lemon wedges.
11. Serve warm.

Herb Lemon Mussels

Servings: 6
Cooking Time: 10 Minutes

Ingredients:

- 1kg mussels, steamed & half shell
- 1 tbsp thyme, chopped
- 1 tbsp parsley, chopped
- 1 tsp dried parsley
- 1 tsp garlic, minced
- 60ml olive oil
- 45ml lemon juice
- Pepper
- Salt

Directions:

1. In a bowl, mix mussels with the remaining ingredients.
2. Insert a crisper plate in the Tower air fryer baskets.
3. Add the mussels to both baskets.
4. Select zone 1 then select "air fry" mode and set the temperature to 360 degrees F for 10 minutes. Press "match" to match zone 2 settings to zone 1. Press "start/stop" to begin.

Nutrition:

- (Per serving) Calories 206 | Fat 11.9g |Sodium 462mg | Carbs 6.3g | Fiber 0.3g | Sugar 0.2g | Protein 18.2g

Bang Bang Shrimp

Servings: 4
Cooking Time: 20 Minutes
Ingredients:

- For the shrimp:
- 1 cup corn starch
- Salt and pepper, to taste
- 2 pounds shrimp, peeled and deveined
- ½ to 1 cup buttermilk
- Cooking oil spray
- 1 large egg whisked with 1 teaspoon water
- For the sauce:
- ⅓ cup sweet Thai chili sauce
- ¼ cup sour cream
- ¼ cup mayonnaise
- 2 tablespoons buttermilk
- 1 tablespoon sriracha, or to taste
- Pinch dried dill weed

Directions:

1. Season the corn starch with salt and pepper in a wide, shallow bowl.
2. In a large mixing bowl, toss the shrimp in the buttermilk to coat them.
3. Dredge the shrimp in the seasoned corn starch.
4. Brush with the egg wash after spraying with cooking oil.
5. Place a crisper plate in each drawer. Place the shrimp in a single layer in each. You may need to cook in batches.
6. Select zone 1, then AIR FRY, then set the temperature to 360 degrees F/ 180 degrees C with a 5-minute timer. To match zone 2 settings to zone 1, choose MATCH. To begin, select START/STOP.
7. Meanwhile, combine all the sauce ingredients together in a bowl.
8. Remove the shrimp when the cooking time is over.

Nutrition:

- (Per serving) Calories 415 | Fat 15g | Sodium 1875mg | Carbs 28g | Fiber 1g | Sugar 5g | Protein 38g

Flavorful Salmon Fillets

Servings: 2
Cooking Time:10 Minutes
Ingredients:

- 2 salmon fillets, boneless
- 1/2 tsp garlic powder
- 1/2 tsp ground cumin
- 1/2 tsp chili powder
- 2 tbsp fresh lemon juice
- 2 tbsp olive oil
- Pepper
- Salt

Directions:

1. In a small bowl, mix oil, lemon juice, chili powder, ground cumin, garlic powder, pepper, and salt.
2. Brush salmon fillets with oil mixture and place into the air fryer basket and cook at 400 F for 10 minutes.
3. Serve and enjoy.

Stuffed Mushrooms With Crab

Servings: 4
Cooking Time: 18 Minutes

Ingredients:

- 907g baby bella mushrooms
- cooking spray
- 2 teaspoons tony chachere's salt blend
- ¼ red onion, diced
- 2 celery ribs, diced
- 227g lump crab
- ½ cup seasoned bread crumbs
- 1 large egg
- ½ cup parmesan cheese, shredded
- 1 teaspoon oregano
- 1 teaspoon hot sauce

Directions:

1. Mix all the ingredients except the mushrooms in a bowl.
2. Divide the crab filling into the mushroom caps.
3. Place the caps in the air fryer baskets.
4. Return the air fryer basket 1 to Zone 1, and basket 2 to Zone 2 of the Tower 2-Basket Air Fryer.
5. Choose the "Air Fry" mode for Zone 1 at 400 degrees F and 18 minutes of cooking time.
6. Select the "MATCH COOK" option to copy the settings for Zone 2.
7. Initiate cooking by pressing the START/PAUSE BUTTON.
8. Serve warm.

Nutrition:

- (Per serving) Calories 399 | Fat 16g |Sodium 537mg | Carbs 28g | Fiber 3g | Sugar 10g | Protein 35g

Honey Teriyaki Tilapia

Servings: 4
Cooking Time: 10 Minutes

Ingredients:

- 8 tablespoons low-sodium teriyaki sauce
- 3 tablespoons honey
- 2 garlic cloves, minced
- 2 tablespoons extra virgin olive oil
- 3 pieces tilapia (each cut into 2 pieces)

Directions:

1. Combine all the first 4 ingredients to make the marinade.
2. Pour the marinade over the tilapia and let it sit for 20 minutes.
3. Place a crisper plate in each drawer. Place the tilapia in the drawers. Insert the drawers into the unit.
4. Select zone 1, then AIR FRY, then set the temperature to 360 degrees F/ 180 degrees C with a 10-minute timer. To match zone 2 settings to zone 1, choose MATCH. To begin, select START/STOP.
5. Remove the tilapia from the drawers after the timer has finished.

Nutrition:

- (Per serving) Calories 350 | Fat 16.4g | Sodium 706mg | Carbs 19.3g | Fiber 0.1g | Sugar 19g | Protein 29.3g

Italian Baked Cod

Servings: 4
Cooking Time: 12 Minutes
Ingredients:

- 4 cod fillets, 170 g each
- 2 tablespoons salted butter, melted
- 1 teaspoon Italian seasoning
- ¼ teaspoon salt
- 120 ml tomato-based pasta sauce

Directions:

1. Place cod into an ungreased round nonstick baking dish. Pour butter over cod and sprinkle with Italian seasoning and salt. Top with pasta sauce.
2. Place dish into the two air fryer drawers. Adjust the temperature to 176°C and bake for 12 minutes. Fillets will be lightly browned, easily flake, and have an internal temperature of at least 64°C when done. Serve warm.

Codfish With Herb Vinaigrette

Servings:2
Cooking Time:16
Ingredients:

- Vinaigrette Ingredients:
- 1/2 cup parsley leaves
- 1 cup basil leaves
- ½ cup mint leaves
- 2 tablespoons thyme leaves
- 1/4 teaspoon red pepper flakes
- 2 cloves of garlic
- 4 tablespoons of red wine vinegar
- ¼ cup of olive oil
- Salt, to taste
- Other Ingredients:
- 1.5 pounds fish fillets, cod fish
- 2 tablespoons olive oil
- Salt and black pepper, to taste
- 1 teaspoon of paprika
- 1teasbpoon of Italian seasoning

Directions:

1. Blend the entire vinaigrette ingredient in a high-speed blender and pulse into a smooth paste.
2. Set aside for drizzling overcooked fish.
3. Rub the fillets with salt, black pepper, paprika, Italian seasoning, and olive oil.
4. Divide it between two baskets of the air fryer.
5. Set the zone 1 to 16 minutes at 390 degrees F, at AIR FRY mode.
6. Press the MATCH button for the second basket.
7. Once done, serve the fillets with the drizzle of blended vinaigrette

Nutrition:

- (Per serving) Calories 1219| Fat 81.8g| Sodium 1906mg | Carbs64.4 g | Fiber5.5 g | Sugar 0.4g | Protein 52.1g

Dukkah-crusted Halibut

Servings: 2

Cooking Time: 17 Minutes

Ingredients:

- Dukkah:
- 1 tablespoon coriander seeds
- 1 tablespoon sesame seeds
- 1½ teaspoons cumin seeds
- 50 g roasted mixed nuts
- ¼ teaspoon kosher or coarse sea salt
- ¼ teaspoon black pepper
- Fish:
- 2 halibut fillets, 140 g each
- 2 tablespoons mayonnaise
- Vegetable oil spray
- Lemon wedges, for serving

Directions:

1. For the Dukkah: Combine the coriander, sesame seeds, and cumin in a small baking pan. Place the pan in the zone 1 air fryer basket. Set the air fryer to 205°C for 5 minutes. Toward the end of the cooking time, you will hear the seeds popping. Transfer to a plate and let cool for 5 minutes. 2. Transfer the toasted seeds to a food processor or spice grinder and add the mixed nuts. Pulse until coarsely chopped. Add the salt and pepper and stir well.
2. 3. For the fish: Spread each fillet with 1 tablespoon of the mayonnaise. Press a heaping tablespoon of the Dukkah into the mayonnaise on each fillet, pressing lightly to adhere. 4. Spray the zone 2 air fryer basket with vegetable oil spray. Place the fish in the zone 2 basket. Cook for 12 minutes, or until the fish flakes easily with a fork. 5. Serve the fish with lemon wedges.

Salmon With Coconut

Servings:2

Cooking Time:15

Ingredients:

- Oil spray, for greasing
- 2 salmon fillets, 6ounces each
- Salt and ground black pepper, to taste
- 1 tablespoon butter, for frying
- 1 tablespoon red curry paste
- 1 cup of coconut cream
- 2 tablespoons fresh cilantro, chopped
- 1 cup of cauliflower florets
- ½ cup Parmesan cheese, hard

Directions:

1. Take a bowl and mix salt, black pepper, butter, red curry paste, coconut cream in a bowl and marinate the salmon in it.
2. Oil sprays the cauliflower florets and then seasons it with salt and freshly ground black pepper.
3. Put the florets in the zone 1 basket.
4. Layer the parchment paper over the zone 2 baskets, and then place the salmon fillet on it.
5. Set the zone 2 basket to AIR FRY mod at 15 minutes for4 00 degrees F
6. Hit the smart finish button to finish it at the same time.
7. Once the time for cooking is over, serve the salmon with cauliflower floret with Parmesan cheese drizzle on top.

Nutrition:

- (Per serving) Calories 774 | Fat 59g| Sodium 1223mg | Carbs 12.2g | Fiber 3.9g | Sugar5.9 g | Protein53.5 g

Beef, Pork, And Lamb Recipes

Panko Crusted Calf's Liver Strips

Servings: 4
Cooking Time: 23 To 25 Minutes
Ingredients:

- 450 g sliced calf's liver, cut into ½-inch wide strips
- 2 eggs
- 2 tablespoons milk
- 120 ml whole wheat flour
- 475 ml panko breadcrumbs
- Salt and ground black pepper, to taste
- Cooking spray

Directions:

1. Preheat the air fryer to 200°C and spritz with cooking spray.
2. Rub the calf's liver strips with salt and ground black pepper on a clean work surface.
3. Whisk the eggs with milk in a large bowl. Pour the flour in a shallow dish. Pour the panko on a separate shallow dish.
4. Dunk the liver strips in the flour, then in the egg mixture. Shake the excess off and roll the strips over the panko to coat well.
5. Arrange the liver strips in a single layer in the two preheated air fryer drawers and spritz with cooking spray.
6. Air fry for 5 minutes or until browned. Flip the strips halfway through.
7. Serve immediately.

Parmesan Pork Chops

Servings: 4
Cooking Time: 15 Minutes.
Ingredients:

- 4 boneless pork chops
- 2 tablespoons olive oil
- ½ cup freshly grated Parmesan
- 1 teaspoon salt
- 1 teaspoon paprika
- 1 teaspoon garlic powder
- 1 teaspoon onion powder
- ½ teaspoon black pepper

Directions:

1. Pat dry the pork chops with a paper towel and rub them with olive oil.
2. Mix parmesan with spices in a medium bowl.
3. Rub the pork chops with Parmesan mixture.
4. Place 2 seasoned pork chops in each of the two crisper plate
5. Return the crisper plate to the Tower Dual Zone Air Fryer.
6. Choose the Air Fry mode for Zone 1 and set the temperature to 390 degrees F and the time to 15 minutes.
7. Select the "MATCH" button to copy the settings for Zone 2.
8. Initiate cooking by pressing the START/STOP button.
9. Flip the pork chops when cooked halfway through, then resume cooking.
10. Serve warm.

Nutrition:

- (Per serving) Calories 396 | Fat 23.2g |Sodium 622mg | Carbs 0.7g | Fiber 0g | Sugar 0g | Protein 45.6g

Gochujang Brisket

Servings: 6

Cooking Time: 55 Minutes.

Ingredients:

- ½ tablespoons sweet paprika
- ½ teaspoon toasted sesame oil
- 2 lbs. beef brisket, cut into 4 pieces
- Salt, to taste
- ⅛ cup Gochujang, Korean chili paste
- Black pepper, to taste
- 1 small onion, diced
- 2 garlic cloves, minced
- 1 teaspoon Asian fish sauce
- 1 ½ tablespoons peanut oil, as needed
- ½ tablespoon fresh ginger, grated
- ¼ teaspoon red chili flakes
- ½ cup of water
- 1 tablespoon ketchup
- 1 tablespoon soy sauce

Directions:

1. Thoroughly rub the beef brisket with olive oil, paprika, chili flakes, black pepper, and salt.
2. Cut the brisket in half, then divide the beef in the two crisper plate.
3. Return the crisper plate to the Tower Dual Zone Air Fryer.
4. Choose the Air Fry mode for Zone 1 and set the temperature to 390 degrees F and the time to 35 minutes.
5. Select the "MATCH" button to copy the settings for Zone 2.
6. Initiate cooking by pressing the START/STOP button.
7. Flip the brisket halfway through, and resume cooking.
8. Meanwhile, heat oil in a skillet and add ginger, onion, and garlic.
9. Sauté for 5 minutes, then add all the remaining ingredients.
10. Cook the mixture for 15 minutes approximately until well thoroughly mixed.
11. Serve the brisket with this sauce on top.

Nutrition:

- (Per serving) Calories 374 | Fat 25g |Sodium 275mg | Carbs 7.3g | Fiber 0g | Sugar 6g | Protein 12.3g

Bbq Pork Spare Ribs

Servings: 8
Cooking Time: 30 Minutes

Ingredients:

- ½ cup honey, divided
- 1½ cups BBQ sauce
- 4 tablespoons tomato ketchup
- 2 tablespoons Worcestershire sauce
- 2 tablespoons low-sodium soy sauce
- 1 teaspoon garlic powder
- Freshly ground white pepper, as required
- 3½ pounds pork ribs

Directions:

1. In a bowl, mix together 6 tablespoons of honey and the remaining ingredients except pork ribs.
2. Add the pork ribs and coat with the mixture generously.
3. Refrigerate to marinate for about 20 minutes.
4. Grease each basket of "Zone 1" and "Zone 2" of Tower 2-Basket Air Fryer.
5. Press "Zone 1" and "Zone 2" and then rotate the knob for each zone to select "Air Fry".
6. Set the temperature to 355 degrees F/ 180 degrees C for both zones and then set the time for 5 minutes to preheat.
7. After preheating, arrange the ribs into the basket of each zone.
8. Slide each basket into Air Fryer and set the time for 26 minutes.
9. While cooking, flip the ribs once halfway through.
10. After cooking time is completed, remove the ribs from Air Fryer and place onto serving plates.
11. Drizzle with the remaining honey and serve immediately.

Air Fried Lamb Chops

Servings: 4
Cooking Time: 10 Minutes

Ingredients:

- 700g lamb chops
- ½ teaspoon oregano
- 3 tablespoons parsley, minced
- ½ teaspoon black pepper
- 3 cloves garlic minced
- 2 tablespoons lemon juice
- 2 tablespoons olive oil
- Salt to taste

Directions:

1. Pat dry the chops and mix with lemon juice and the rest of the ingredients.
2. Place these chops in the air fryer baskets.
3. Return the air fryer basket 1 to Zone 1, and basket 2 to Zone 2 of the Tower 2-Basket Air Fryer.
4. Choose the "Air Fry" mode for Zone 1and set the temperature to 400 degrees F and 10 minutes of cooking time.
5. Select the "MATCH COOK" option to copy the settings for Zone 2.
6. Initiate cooking by pressing the START/PAUSE BUTTON.
7. Flip the pork chops once cooked halfway through.
8. Serve warm.

Meat And Rice Stuffed Peppers

Servings: 4
Cooking Time: 18 Minutes
Ingredients:

- 340 g lean beef mince
- 110 g lean pork mince
- 60 ml onion, minced
- 1 (425 g) can finely-chopped tomatoes
- 1 teaspoon Worcestershire sauce
- 1 teaspoon barbecue seasoning
- 1 teaspoon honey
- ½ teaspoon dried basil
- 120 ml cooked brown rice
- ½ teaspoon garlic powder
- ½ teaspoon oregano
- ½ teaspoon salt
- 2 small peppers, cut in half, stems removed, deseeded
- Cooking spray

Directions:

1. Preheat the zone 1 air fryer drawer to 182°C and spritz a baking pan with cooking spray.
2. Arrange the beef, pork, and onion in the baking pan and bake in the preheated air fryer drawer for 8 minutes. Break the ground meat into chunks halfway through the cooking.
3. Meanwhile, combine the tomatoes, Worcestershire sauce, barbecue seasoning, honey, and basil in a saucepan. Stir to mix well.
4. Transfer the cooked meat mixture to a large bowl and add the cooked rice, garlic powder, oregano, salt, and 60 ml of the tomato mixture. Stir to mix well.
5. Stuff the pepper halves with the mixture, then arrange the pepper halves in the zone 1 air fryer drawer and air fry for 10 minutes or until the peppers are lightly charred.
6. Serve the stuffed peppers with the remaining tomato sauce on top.

Honey-baked Pork Loin

Servings: 6
Cooking Time: 22 To 25 Minutes
Ingredients:

- 60 ml honey
- 60 ml freshly squeezed lemon juice
- 2 tablespoons soy sauce
- 1 teaspoon garlic powder
- 1 (900 g) pork loin
- 2 tablespoons vegetable oil

Directions:

1. In a medium bowl, whisk together the honey, lemon juice, soy sauce, and garlic powder. Reserve half of the mixture for basting during cooking.
2. Cut 5 slits in the pork loin and transfer it to a resealable bag. Add the remaining honey mixture. Seal the bag and refrigerate to marinate for at least 2 hours.
3. Preheat the air fryer to 204°C. Line the two air fryer drawers with parchment paper.
4. Remove the pork from the marinade, and place it on the parchment. Spritz with oil, then baste with the reserved marinade.
5. Cook for 15 minutes. Flip the pork, baste with more marinade and spritz with oil again. Cook for 7 to 10 minutes more until the internal temperature reaches 64°C. Let rest for 5 minutes before serving.

Ham Burger Patties

Servings:2

Cooking Time:17

Ingredients:

- 1 pound of ground beef
- Salt and pepper, to taste
- ½ teaspoon of red chili powder
- ¼ teaspoon of coriander powder
- 2 tablespoons of chopped onion
- 1 green chili, chopped
- Oil spray for greasing
- 2 large potato wedges

Directions:

1. Oil greases the air fryer baskets with oil spray.
2. Add potato wedges in the zone 1 basket.
3. Take a bowl and add minced beef in it and add salt, pepper, chili powder, coriander powder, green chili, and chopped onion.
4. mix well and make two burger patties with wet hands place the two patties in the air fryer zone 2 basket.
5. put the basket inside the air fryer.
6. now, set time for zone 1 for 12 minutes using AIR FRY mode at 400 degrees F.
7. Select the MATCH button for zone 2.
8. once the time of cooking complete, take out the baskets.
9. flip the patties and shake the potatoes wedges.
10. again, set time of zone 1 basket for 4 minutes at 400 degrees F
11. Select the MATCH button for the second basket.
12. Once it's done, serve and enjoy.

Nutrition:

- (Per serving) Calories875 | Fat21.5g | Sodium 622mg | Carbs 88g | Fiber10.9 g| Sugar 3.4g | Protein 78.8g

Italian Sausage And Cheese Meatballs

Servings: 4

Cooking Time: 20 Minutes

Ingredients:

- 230 g sausage meat with Italian seasoning added to taste
- 230 g 85% lean beef mince
- 120 ml shredded sharp Cheddar cheese
- ½ teaspoon onion granules
- ½ teaspoon garlic powder
- ½ teaspoon black pepper

Directions:

1. In a large bowl, gently mix the sausage meat, beef mince, cheese, onion granules, garlic powder, and pepper until well combined.
2. Form the mixture into 16 meatballs. Place the meatballs in a single layer in the two air fryer drawers. Set the air fryer to 176°C for 20 minutes, turning the meatballs halfway through the cooking time. Use a meat thermometer to ensure the meatballs have reached an internal temperature of 72°C .

Spicy Bavette Steak With Zhoug

Servings: 4

Cooking Time: 8 Minutes

Ingredients:

- Marinade and Steak:
- 120 ml dark beer or orange juice
- 60 ml fresh lemon juice
- 3 cloves garlic, minced
- 2 tablespoons extra-virgin olive oil
- 2 tablespoons Sriracha
- 2 tablespoons brown sugar
- 2 teaspoons ground cumin
- 2 teaspoons smoked paprika
- 1 tablespoon coarse or flaky salt
- 1 teaspoon black pepper
- 680 g bavette or skirt steak, trimmed and cut into 3 pieces
- Zhoug:
- 235 ml packed fresh coriander leaves
- 2 cloves garlic, peeled
- 2 jalapeño or green chiles, stemmed and coarsely chopped
- ½ teaspoon ground cumin
- ¼ teaspoon ground coriander
- ¼ teaspoon coarse or flaky salt
- 2 to 4 tablespoons extra-virgin olive oil

Directions:

1. For the marinade and steak: In a small bowl, whisk together the beer, lemon juice, garlic, olive oil, Sriracha, brown sugar, cumin, paprika, salt, and pepper. Place the steak in a large resealable plastic bag. Pour the marinade over the steak, seal the bag, and massage the steak to coat. Marinate in the refrigerator for 1 hour or up to 24 hours, turning the bag occasionally. 2. Meanwhile, for the zhoug: In a food processor, combine the coriander, garlic, jalapeños, cumin, coriander, and salt. Process until finely chopped. Add 2 tablespoons olive oil and pulse to form a loose paste, adding up to 2 tablespoons more olive oil if needed. Transfer the zhoug to a glass container. Cover and store in the refrigerator until 30 minutes before serving if marinating more than 1 hour. 3. Remove the steak from the marinade and discard the marinade. Place the steak in the zone 1 air fryer drawer and set the temperature to 204°C for 8 minutes. Use a meat thermometer to ensure the steak has reached an internal temperature of 64°C . 4. Transfer the steak to a cutting board and let rest for 5 minutes. Slice the steak across the grain and serve with the zhoug.

Chipotle Beef

Servings: 4
Cooking Time: 18 Minutes.

Ingredients:

- 1 lb. beef steak, cut into chunks
- 1 large egg
- ½ cup parmesan cheese, grated
- ½ cup pork panko
- ½ teaspoon seasoned salt
- Chipotle Ranch Dip
- ¼ cup mayonnaise
- ¼ cup sour cream
- 1 teaspoon chipotle paste
- ½ teaspoon ranch dressing mix
- ¼ medium lime, juiced

Directions:

1. Mix all the ingredients for chipotle ranch dip in a bowl.
2. Keep it in the refrigerator for 30 minutes.
3. Mix pork panko with salt and parmesan.
4. Beat egg in one bowl and spread the panko mixture in another flat bowl.
5. Dip the steak chunks in the egg first, then coat them with panko mixture.
6. Spread them in the two crisper plates and spray them with cooking oil.
7. Return the crisper plate to the Tower Dual Zone Air Fryer.
8. Choose the Air Fry mode for Zone 1 and set the temperature to 390 degrees F and the time to 18 minutes.
9. Select the "MATCH" button to copy the settings for Zone 2.
10. Initiate cooking by pressing the START/STOP button.
11. Serve with chipotle ranch and salt and pepper on top. Enjoy.

Nutrition:

- (Per serving) Calories 310 | Fat 17g |Sodium 271mg | Carbs 4.3g | Fiber 0.9g | Sugar 2.1g | Protein 35g

Bbq Pork Chops

Servings: 4
Cooking Time: 12 Minutes

Ingredients:

- 4 pork chops
- Salt and black pepper to taste
- 1 package BBQ Shake & Bake
- Olive oil

Directions:

1. Season pork chops with black pepper, salt, BBQ shake and olive oil.
2. Place these chops in the air fryer baskets.
3. Return the air fryer basket 1 to Zone 1, and basket 2 to Zone 2 of the Tower 2-Basket Air Fryer.
4. Choose the "Air Fry" mode for Zone 1 at 375 degrees F and 12 minutes of cooking time.
5. Select the "MATCH COOK" option to copy the settings for Zone 2.
6. Initiate cooking by pressing the START/PAUSE BUTTON.
7. Flip the pork chops once cooked halfway through.
8. Serve warm.

Mustard Rubbed Lamb Chops

Servings: 4
Cooking Time: 31 Minutes.
Ingredients:

- 1 teaspoon Dijon mustard
- 1 teaspoon olive oil
- ½ teaspoon soy sauce
- ½ teaspoon garlic, minced
- ½ teaspoon cumin powder
- ½ teaspoon cayenne pepper
- ½ teaspoon Italian spice blend
- ⅛ teaspoon salt
- 4 pieces of lamb chops

Directions:

1. Mix Dijon mustard, soy sauce, olive oil, garlic, cumin powder, cayenne pepper, Italian spice blend, and salt in a medium bowl and mix well.
2. Place lamb chops into a Ziploc bag and pour in the marinade.
3. Press the air out of the bag and seal tightly.
4. Press the marinade around the lamb chops to coat.
5. Keep then in the fridge and marinate for at least 30 minutes, up to overnight.
6. Place 2 chops in each of the crisper plate and spray them with cooking oil.
7. Return the crisper plate to the Tower Dual Zone Air Fryer.
8. Select the Roast mode for Zone 1 and set the temperature to 350 degrees F and the time to 27 minutes.
9. Select the "MATCH" button to copy the settings for Zone 2.
10. Initiate cooking by pressing the START/STOP button.
11. Flip the chops once cooked halfway through, and resume cooking.
12. Switch the Roast mode to Max Crisp mode and cook for 5 minutes.
13. Serve warm.

Nutrition:

- (Per serving) Calories 264 | Fat 17g |Sodium 129mg | Carbs 0.9g | Fiber 0.3g | Sugar 0g | Protein 27g

Roast Beef

Servings: 4
Cooking Time: 35 Minutes
Ingredients:

- 2 pounds beef roast
- 1 tablespoon olive oil
- 1 medium onion (optional)
- 1 teaspoon salt
- 2 teaspoons rosemary and thyme, chopped (fresh or dried)

Directions:

1. Combine the sea salt, rosemary, and oil in a large, shallow dish.
2. Using paper towels, pat the meat dry. Place it on a dish and turn it to coat the outside with the oil-herb mixture.
3. Peel the onion and split it in half (if using).
4. Install a crisper plate in both drawers. Place half the beef roast and half an onion in the zone 1 drawer and half the beef and half the onion in zone 2's, then insert the drawers into the unit.
5. Select zone 1, select AIR FRY, set temperature to 360 degrees F/ 180 degrees C, and set time to 22 minutes. Select MATCH to match zone 2 settings to zone 1. Press the START/STOP button to begin cooking.
6. When the time reaches 11 minutes, press START/STOP to pause the unit. Remove the drawers and flip the roast. Re-insert the drawers into the unit and press START/STOP to resume cooking.

Nutrition:

- (Per serving) Calories 463 | Fat 17.8g | Sodium 732mg | Carbs 2.8g | Fiber 0.7g | Sugar 1.2g | Protein 69g

Pork Chops With Broccoli

Servings: 2
Cooking Time: 13 Minutes.
Ingredients:

- 2 (5 ounces) bone-in pork chops
- 2 tablespoons avocado oil
- ½ teaspoon paprika
- ½ teaspoon onion powder
- ½ teaspoon garlic powder
- 1 teaspoon salt
- 2 cups broccoli florets
- 2 garlic cloves, minced

Directions:

1. Rub the pork chops with avocado oil, garlic, paprika, and spices.
2. Add pork chop to the crisper plate of Zone 1 in the Tower Dual Zone Air Fryer.
3. Return the crisper plate to the Air Fryer.
4. Choose the Air Fry mode for Zone 1 and set the temperature to 400 degrees F and the time to 12 minutes.
5. Add the broccoli to the Zone 2 drawer and return it to the unit.
6. Choose the Air Fry mode for Zone 2 with 375 degrees F and the time to 13 minutes.
7. Press the SYNC button to sync the finish time for both Zones.
8. Initiate cooking by pressing the START/STOP button.
9. Flip the pork once cooked halfway through.
10. Cut the hardened butter into the cubes and place them on top of the pork chops.
11. Serve warm with crispy broccoli florets

Nutrition:

- (Per serving) Calories 410 | Fat 17.8g |Sodium 619mg | Carbs 21g | Fiber 1.4g | Sugar 1.8g | Protein 38.4g

Honey Glazed Bbq Pork Ribs

Servings: 4
Cooking Time: 30 Minutes
Ingredients:

- 2 pounds pork ribs
- ¼ cup honey, divided
- 1 cup BBQ sauce
- ½ teaspoon garlic powder
- 2 tablespoons tomato ketchup
- 1 tablespoon Worcestershire sauce
- 1 tablespoon low-sodium soy sauce
- Freshly ground white pepper, as required

Directions:

1. In a bowl, mix together honey and the remaining ingredients except pork ribs.
2. Add the pork ribs and coat with the mixture generously.
3. Refrigerate to marinate for about 20 minutes.
4. Grease each basket of "Zone 1" and "Zone 2" of Tower 2-Basket Air Fryer.
5. Press "Zone 1" and "Zone 2" and then rotate the knob for each zone to select "Air Fry".
6. Set the temperature to 355 degrees F/ 180 degrees C for both zones and then set the time for 5 minutes to preheat.
7. After preheating, arrange the ribs into the basket of each zone.
8. Slide each basket into Air Fryer and set the time for 26 minutes.
9. While cooking, flip the ribs once halfway through.
10. After cooking time is completed, remove the ribs from Air Fryer and place onto serving plates.
11. Drizzle with the remaining honey and serve immediately.

Roast Souvlaki-style Pork With Lemon-feta Baby Potatoes

Servings:4
Cooking Time: 40 Minutes

Ingredients:

- FOR THE PORK
- 1½ pounds pork tenderloin, cut into bite-size cubes
- ¼ cup olive oil
- ¼ cup fresh lemon juice
- 2 teaspoons minced garlic
- 2 teaspoons honey
- 1½ teaspoons dried oregano
- ¼ teaspoon kosher salt
- ¼ teaspoon freshly ground black pepper
- FOR THE POTATOES
- 1 pound baby red or yellow potatoes, halved
- 1 tablespoon olive oil
- Grated zest and juice of 1 lemon
- ½ teaspoon kosher salt
- ¼ teaspoon freshly ground black pepper
- ⅓ cup crumbled feta cheese
- 2 tablespoons chopped fresh parsley

Directions:

1. To prep the pork: In a large bowl, combine the pork, oil, lemon juice, garlic, honey, oregano, salt, and black pepper. If desired, cover and refrigerate up to 24 hours.
2. To prep the potatoes: In a large bowl, combine the potatoes, oil, lemon zest, lemon juice, salt, and black pepper. Mix to coat the potatoes.
3. To cook the pork and potatoes: Install a crisper plate in each of the two baskets. Place the pork in the Zone 1 basket and insert the basket in the unit. Place the potatoes in the Zone 2 basket and insert the basket in the unit.
4. Select Zone 1, select ROAST, set the temperature to 390°F, and set the time to 20 minutes.
5. Select Zone 2, select AIR FRY, set the temperature to 400°F, and set the time to 40 minutes. Select SMART FINISH.
6. Press START/PAUSE to begin cooking.
7. When cooking is complete, the pork will be cooked through (an instant-read thermometer should read 145°F) and the potatoes will be tender and beginning to brown around the edges.
8. Stir the feta and parsley into the potatoes. Serve the pork and potatoes while hot.

Nutrition:

- (Per serving) Calories: 395; Total fat: 17g; Saturated fat: 4.5g; Carbohydrates: 24g; Fiber: 2g; Protein: 37g; Sodium: 399mg

Zucchini Pork Skewers

Servings: 4
Cooking Time: 23 Minutes.

Ingredients:

- 1 large zucchini, cut 1" pieces
- 1 lb. boneless pork belly, cut into cubes
- 1 onion yellow, diced in squares
- 1 ½ cups grape tomatoes
- 1 garlic clove minced
- 1 lemon, juice only
- ¼ cup olive oil
- 2 tablespoons balsamic vinegar
- 1 teaspoon oregano
- olive oil spray

Directions:

1. Mix together balsamic vinegar, garlic, oregano lemon juice, and ¼ cup of olive oil in a suitable bowl.
2. Then toss in diced pork pieces and mix well to coat.
3. Leave the seasoned pork to marinate for 60 minutes in the refrigerator.
4. Take suitable wooden skewers for your Tower Dual Zone Air Fryer's drawer, and then thread marinated pork and vegetables on each skewer in an alternating manner.
5. Place half of the skewers in each of the crisper plate and spray them with cooking oil.
6. Return the crisper plate to the Tower Dual Zone Air Fryer.
7. Choose the Air Fry mode for Zone 1 and set the temperature to 390 degrees F and the time to 23 minutes.
8. Select the "MATCH" button to copy the settings for Zone 2.
9. Initiate cooking by pressing the START/STOP button.
10. Flip the skewers once cooked halfway through, and resume cooking.
11. Serve warm.

Nutrition:

- (Per serving) Calories 459 | Fat 17.7g |Sodium 1516mg | Carbs 1.7g | Fiber 0.5g | Sugar 0.4g | Protein 69.2g

Pigs In A Blanket And Currywurst

Servings: 6
Cooking Time: 12 Minutes

Ingredients:

- Pigs in a Blanket:
- 120 ml shredded Mozzarella cheese
- 2 tablespoons blanched finely ground almond flour
- 30 g full-fat cream cheese
- 2 (110 g) beef smoked sausage, cut in two
- ½ teaspoon sesame seeds
- Currywurst:
- 235 ml tomato sauce
- 2 tablespoons cider vinegar
- 2 teaspoons curry powder
- 2 teaspoons sweet paprika
- 1 teaspoon sugar
- ¼ teaspoon cayenne pepper

- 1 small onion, diced
- 450 g bratwurst, sliced diagonally into 1-inch pieces

Directions:

1. Make the Pigs in a Blanket : Place Mozzarella, almond flour, and cream cheese in a large microwave-safe bowl. Microwave for 45 seconds and stir until smooth. Roll dough into a ball and cut in half. 2. Press each half out into a 4 × 5-inch rectangle. Roll one sausage up in each dough half and press seams closed. Sprinkle the top with sesame seeds. 3. Place each wrapped sausage into the zone 1 air fryer drawer. 4. Adjust the temperature to 204°C and air fry for 7 minutes. 5. The outside will be golden when completely cooked. Serve immediately.
2. Make the Currywurst : 1. In a large bowl, combine the tomato sauce, vinegar, curry powder, paprika, sugar, and cayenne. Whisk until well combined. Stir in the onion and bratwurst. Transfer the mixture to a baking pan. Place the pan in the zone 2 air fryer drawer. Set the temperature to 204°C for 12 minutes, or until the sausage is heated through and the sauce is bubbling.

Lamb Chops With Dijon Garlic

Servings: 4

Cooking Time: 22 Minutes

Ingredients:

- 2 teaspoons Dijon mustard
- 2 teaspoons olive oil
- 1 teaspoon soy sauce
- 1 teaspoon garlic, minced
- 1 teaspoon cumin powder
- 1 teaspoon cayenne pepper
- 1 teaspoon Italian spice blend (optional)
- ¼ teaspoon salt
- 8 lamb chops

Directions:

1. Combine the Dijon mustard, olive oil, soy sauce, garlic, cumin powder, cayenne pepper, Italian spice blend (optional), and salt in a medium mixing bowl.
2. Put the marinade in a large Ziploc bag. Add the lamb chops. Seal the bag tightly after pressing out the air. Coat the lamb in the marinade by shaking the bag and pressing the chops into the mixture. Place in the fridge for at least 30 minutes, or up to overnight, to marinate.
3. Install a crisper plate in both drawers. Place half the lamb chops in the zone 1 drawer and half in zone 2's, then insert the drawers into the unit.
4. Select zone 1, select AIR FRY, set temperature to 390 degrees F/ 200 degrees C, and set time to 22 minutes. Select MATCH to match zone 2 settings to zone 1. Press the START/STOP button to begin cooking.
5. When the time reaches 11 minutes, press START/STOP to pause the unit. Remove the drawers and flip the lamb chops. Re-insert the drawers into the unit and press START/STOP to resume cooking.
6. Serve and enjoy!

Nutrition:

- (Per serving) Calories 343 | Fat 15.1g | Sodium 380mg | Carbs 0.9 g | Fiber 0.3g | Sugar 0.1g | Protein 48.9g

Poultry Recipes

Chicken Breast Strips

Servings:2
Cooking Time:22
Ingredients:

- 2 large organic egg
- 1-ounce buttermilk
- 1 cup of cornmeal
- ¼ cup all-purpose flour
- Salt and black pepper, to taste
- 1 pound of chicken breasts, cut into strips
- 2 tablespoons of oil bay seasoning
- oil spray, for greasing

Directions:

1. Take a medium bowl and whisk eggs with buttermilk.
2. In a separate large bowl mix flour, cornmeal, salt, black pepper, and oil bay seasoning.
3. First, dip the chicken breast strip in egg wash and then dredge into the flour mixture.
4. Coat the strip all over and layer on both the baskets that are already grease with oil spray.
5. Grease the chicken breast strips with oil spray as well.
6. Set the zone 1 basket to AIR FRY mode at 400 degrees F for 22 minutes.
7. Select the MATCH button for zone 2.
8. Hit the start button to let the cooking start.
9. Once the cooking cycle is done, serve.

Nutrition:

- (Per serving) Calories 788| Fat25g| Sodium835 mg | Carbs60g | Fiber 4.9g| Sugar1.5g | Protein79g

Asian Chicken Drumsticks

Servings: 4
Cooking Time: 20 Minutes
Ingredients:

- 8 chicken drumsticks
- 1 lime juice
- 30ml rice wine
- 45ml fish sauce
- 2 tbsp garlic, minced
- 55g brown sugar
- ½ tsp Sriracha sauce
- 1 tsp black pepper
- 1 tsp sesame oil
- Salt

Directions:

1. Add chicken drumsticks and remaining ingredients into the bowl and mix well. Cover and place in refrigerator for 4 hours.
2. Insert a crisper plate in the Tower air fryer baskets.
3. Place the marinated chicken drumsticks in both baskets.
4. Select zone 1, then select "air fry" mode and set the temperature to 360 degrees F for 20 minutes. Press "match" to match zone 2 settings to zone 1. Press "start/stop" to begin.

Nutrition:

- (Per serving) Calories 225 | Fat 6.4g |Sodium 1223mg | Carbs 14.6g | Fiber 0.2g | Sugar 11.3g | Protein 26.3g

Chicken Ranch Wraps

Servings: 4
Cooking Time: 22 Minutes

Ingredients:

- 1½ ounces breaded chicken breast tenders
- 4 (12-inch) whole-wheat tortilla wraps
- 2 heads romaine lettuce, chopped
- ½ cup shredded mozzarella cheese
- 4 tablespoons ranch dressing

Directions:

1. Place a crisper plate in each drawer. Place half of the chicken tenders in one drawer and half in the other. Insert the drawers into thc unit.
2. Select zone 1, then AIR FRY, and set the temperature to 390 degrees F/ 200 degrees C with a 22-minute timer. To match zone 2 settings to zone 1, choose MATCH. To begin cooking, press the START/STOP button.
3. To pause the unit, press START/STOP when the timer reaches 11 minutes. Remove the drawers from the unit and flip the tenders over. To resume cooking, re-insert the drawers into the device and press START/STOP.
4. Remove the chicken from the drawers when they're done cooking and chop them up.
5. Divide the chopped chicken between warmed-up wraps. Top with some lettuce, cheese, and ranch dressing. Wrap and serve.

Nutrition:

- (Per serving) Calories 212 | Fat 7.8g | Sodium 567mg | Carbs 9.1g | Fiber 34.4g | Sugar 9.7g | Protein 10.6g

Chicken Parmesan

Servings: 4
Cooking Time: 10 Minutes

Ingredients:

- Oil, for spraying
- 2 (230 g) boneless, skinless chicken breasts
- 120 g Italian-style bread crumbs
- 20 g grated Parmesan cheese, plus 45 g shredded
- 4 tablespoons unsalted butter, melted
- 115 g marinara sauce

Directions:

1. Preheat the air fryer to 180°C. Line the two air fryer drawers with parchment and spray lightly with oil.
2. Cut each chicken breast in half through its thickness to make 4 thin cutlets. Using a meat tenderizer, pound each cutlet until it is about ¾ inch thick.
3. On a plate, mix together the bread crumbs and grated Parmesan cheese.
4. Lightly brush the chicken with the melted butter, then dip into the bread crumb mixture.
5. Place the chicken in the two prepared drawers and spray lightly with oil.
6. Cook for 6 minutes. Top the chicken with the marinara and shredded Parmesan cheese, dividing evenly. Cook for another 3 to 4 minutes, or until golden brown, crispy, and the internal temperature reaches 76°C.

Curried Orange Honey Chicken

Servings: 4
Cooking Time: 16 To 19 Minutes
Ingredients:

- 340 g boneless, skinless chicken thighs, cut into 1-inch pieces
- 1 yellow bell pepper, cut into 1½-inch pieces
- 1 small red onion, sliced
- Olive oil for misting
- 60 ml chicken stock
- 2 tablespoons honey
- 60 ml orange juice
- 1 tablespoon cornflour
- 2 to 3 teaspoons curry powder

Directions:

1. Preheat the air fryer to 190°C.
2. Put the chicken thighs, pepper, and red onion in the zone 1 air fryer drawer and mist with olive oil.
3. Roast for 12 to 14 minutes or until the chicken is cooked to 76°C, shaking the drawer halfway through cooking time.
4. Remove the chicken and vegetables from the air fryer drawer and set aside.
5. In a metal bowl, combine the stock, honey, orange juice, cornflour, and curry powder, and mix well. Add the chicken and vegetables, stir, and put the bowl in the drawer.
6. Return the drawer to the air fryer and roast for 2 minutes. Remove and stir, then roast for 2 to 3 minutes or until the sauce is thickened and bubbly.
7. Serve warm.

Greek Chicken Souvlaki

Servings: 3 To 4
Cooking Time: 15 Minutes
Ingredients:

- Chicken:
- Grated zest and juice of 1 lemon
- 2 tablespoons extra-virgin olive oil
- 1 tablespoon Greek souvlaki seasoning
- 450 g boneless, skinless chicken breast, cut into 2-inch chunks
- Vegetable oil spray
- For Serving:
- Warm pita bread or hot cooked rice
- Sliced ripe tomatoes
- Sliced cucumbers
- Thinly sliced red onion
- Kalamata olives
- Tzatziki

Directions:

1. For the chicken: In a small bowl, combine the lemon zest, lemon juice, olive oil, and souvlaki seasoning. Place the chicken in a gallon-size resealable plastic bag. Pour the marinade over chicken. Seal bag and massage to coat. Place the bag in a large bowl and marinate for 30 minutes, or cover and refrigerate up to 24 hours, turning the bag occasionally. 2. Place the chicken a single layer in the zone 1 air fryer drawer. Cook at 180°C for 10 minutes, turning the chicken and spraying with a little vegetable oil spray halfway through the cooking time. Increase the air fryer temperature to 200°C for 5 minutes to allow the chicken to crisp and brown a little. 3. Transfer the chicken to a serving platter and serve with pita bread or rice, tomatoes, cucumbers, onion, olives and tzatziki.

Buttermilk Fried Chicken

Servings: 6
Cooking Time: 30 Minutes

Ingredients:

- 1½ pounds boneless, skinless chicken thighs
- 2 cups buttermilk
- 1 cup all-purpose flour
- 1 tablespoon seasoned salt
- ½ tablespoon ground black pepper
- 1 cup panko breadcrumbs
- Cooking spray

Directions:

1. Place the chicken thighs in a shallow baking dish. Cover with the buttermilk. Refrigerate for 4 hours or overnight.
2. In a large gallon-sized resealable bag, combine the flour, seasoned salt, and pepper.
3. Remove the chicken from the buttermilk but don't discard the mixture.
4. Add the chicken to the bag and shake well to coat.
5. Dip the thighs in the buttermilk again, then coat in the panko breadcrumbs.
6. Install a crisper plate in each drawer. Place half the chicken thighs in the zone 1 drawer and half in zone 2's, then insert the drawers into the unit.
7. Select zone 1, select AIR FRY, set temperature to 390 degrees F/ 200 degrees C, and set time to 30 minutes. Select MATCH to match zone 2 settings to zone 1. Press the START/STOP button to begin cooking.
8. When the time reaches 15 minutes, press START/STOP to pause the unit. Remove the drawers and flip the chicken. Re-insert the drawers into the unit and press START/STOP to resume cooking.
9. When cooking is complete, remove the chicken.

Nutrition:

- (Per serving) Calories 335 | Fat 12.8g | Sodium 687mg | Carbs 33.1g | Fiber 0.4g | Sugar 4g | Protein 24.5g

Chicken With Bacon And Tomato

Servings: 4
Cooking Time: 10 Minutes

Ingredients:

- 4 medium-sized skin-on chicken drumsticks
- 1½ teaspoons herbs de Provence
- Salt and pepper, to taste
- 1 tablespoon rice vinegar
- 2 tablespoons olive oil
- 2 garlic cloves, crushed
- 340 g crushed canned tomatoes
- 1 small-size leek, thinly sliced
- 2 slices smoked bacon, chopped

Directions:

1. Sprinkle the chicken drumsticks with herbs de Provence, salt and pepper; then, drizzle them with rice vinegar and olive oil.
2. Cook in the baking pan at 180°C for 8 to 10 minutes. Pause the air fryer; stir in the remaining ingredients and continue to cook for 15 minutes longer; make sure to check them periodically. Bon appétit!

Spicy Chicken Sandwiches With "fried" Pickles

Servings: 4
Cooking Time: 18 Minutes

Ingredients:

- FOR THE CHICKEN SANDWICHES
- 2 tablespoons all-purpose flour
- 2 large eggs
- 2 teaspoons Louisiana-style hot sauce
- 1 cup panko bread crumbs
- 1 teaspoon paprika
- ½ teaspoon garlic powder
- ¼ teaspoon salt
- ¼ teaspoon freshly ground black pepper
- ¼ teaspoon cayenne pepper (optional)
- 4 thin-sliced chicken cutlets (4 ounces each)
- 2 teaspoons vegetable oil
- 4 hamburger rolls
- FOR THE PICKLES
- 1 cup dill pickle chips, drained
- 1 large egg
- ½ cup panko bread crumbs
- Nonstick cooking spray
- ½ cup ranch dressing, for serving (optional)

Directions:

1. To prep the sandwiches:
2. Set up a breading station with three small shallow bowls. Place the flour in the first bowl. In the second bowl, whisk together the eggs and hot sauce. Combine the panko, paprika, garlic powder, salt, black pepper, and cayenne pepper in the third bowl.
3. Bread the chicken cutlets in this order: First, dip them into the flour, coating both sides. Then, dip into the egg mixture. Finally, coat them in the panko mixture, gently pressing the breading into the chicken to help it adhere. Drizzle the cutlets with the oil.
4. To prep the pickles:
5. Pat the pickles dry with a paper towel.
6. In a small shallow bowl, whisk the egg. Add the panko to a second shallow bowl.
7. Dip the pickles in the egg, then the panko. Mist both sides of the pickles with cooking spray.
8. To cook the chicken and pickles:
9. Install a crisper plate in each of the two baskets. Place the chicken in the Zone 1 basket and insert the basket in the unit. Place the pickles in the Zone 2 basket and insert the basket in the unit.
10. Select Zone 1, select AIR FRY, set the temperature to 390°F, and set the time to 18 minutes.
11. Select Zone 2, select AIR FRY, set the temperature to 400°F, and set the time to 15 minutes. Select SMART FINISH.
12. Press START/PAUSE to begin cooking.
13. When both timers read 10 minutes, press START/PAUSE. Remove the Zone 1 basket and use silicone-tipped tongs to flip the chicken. Reinsert the basket. Remove the Zone 2 basket and shake to redistribute the pickles. Reinsert the basket and press START/PAUSE to resume cooking.
14. When cooking is complete, the breading will be crisp and golden brown and the chicken cooked through . Place one chicken cutlet on each hamburger roll. Serve the "fried" pickles on the side with ranch dressing, if desired.

"fried" Chicken With Warm Baked Potato Salad

Servings: 4
Cooking Time: 40 Minutes
Ingredients:

- FOR THE "FRIED" CHICKEN
- 1 cup buttermilk
- 1 tablespoon kosher salt
- 4 bone-in, skin-on chicken drumsticks and/or thighs
- 2 cups all-purpose flour
- 1 tablespoon seasoned salt
- 1 tablespoon paprika
- Nonstick cooking spray
- FOR THE POTATO SALAD
- 1½ pounds baby red potatoes, halved
- 1 tablespoon vegetable oil
- ½ cup mayonnaise
- ⅓ cup plain reduced-fat Greek yogurt
- 1 tablespoon apple cider vinegar
- ½ teaspoon kosher salt
- ½ teaspoon freshly ground black pepper
- ¾ cup shredded Cheddar cheese
- 4 slices cooked bacon, crumbled
- 3 scallions, sliced

Directions:

1. To prep the chicken:
2. In a large bowl, combine the buttermilk and salt. Add the chicken and turn to coat. Let rest for at least 30 minutes .
3. In a separate large bowl, combine the flour, seasoned salt, and paprika.
4. Remove the chicken from the marinade and allow any excess marinade to drip off. Discard the marinade. Dip the chicken pieces in the flour, coating them thoroughly. Mist with cooking spray. Let the chicken rest for 10 minutes.
5. To prep the potatoes: In a large bowl, combine the potatoes and oil and toss to coat.
6. To cook the chicken and potatoes:
7. Install a crisper plate in the Zone 1 basket. Place the chicken in the basket in a single layer and insert the basket in the unit. Place the potatoes in the Zone 2 basket and insert the basket in the unit.
8. Select Zone 1, select AIR FRY, set the temperature to 390°F, and set the time to 30 minutes.
9. Select Zone 2, select BAKE, set the temperature to 400°F, and set the time to 40 minutes. Select SMART FINISH.
10. Press START/PAUSE to begin cooking.
11. When cooking is complete, the chicken will be golden brown and cooked through and the potatoes will be fork-tender.
12. Rinse the potatoes under cold water for about 1 minute to cool them.
13. Place the potatoes in a large bowl and stir in the mayonnaise, yogurt, vinegar, salt, and black pepper. Gently stir in the Cheddar, bacon, and scallions. Serve warm with the "fried" chicken.

Chicken Strips With Satay Sauce

Servings: 4
Cooking Time: 10 Minutes
Ingredients:

- 4 (170 g) boneless, skinless chicken breasts, sliced into 16 (1-inch) strips
- 1 teaspoon fine sea salt
- 1 teaspoon paprika
- Sauce:
- 60 g creamy almond butter (or sunflower seed butter for nut-free)
- 2 tablespoons chicken broth
- 1½ tablespoons coconut vinegar or unseasoned rice vinegar
- 1 clove garlic, minced
- 1 teaspoon peeled and minced fresh ginger
- ½ teaspoon hot sauce
- ⅛ teaspoon stevia glycerite, or 2 to 3 drops liquid stevia
- For Garnish/Serving (Optional):
- 15 g chopped coriander leaves
- Red pepper flakes
- Sea salt flakes
- Thinly sliced red, orange, and yellow bell peppers
- Special Equipment:
- 16 wooden or bamboo skewers, soaked in water for 15 minutes

Directions:

1. Spray the zone 1 air fryer drawer with avocado oil. Preheat the air fryer to 200°C. 2. Thread the chicken strips onto the skewers. Season on all sides with the salt and paprika. Place the chicken skewers in the air fryer drawer and air fry for 5 minutes, flip, and cook for another 5 minutes, until the chicken is cooked through and the internal temperature reaches 76°C. 3. While the chicken skewers cook, make the sauce: In a medium-sized bowl, stir together all the sauce ingredients until well combined. Taste and adjust the sweetness and heat to your liking. 4. Garnish the chicken with coriander, red pepper flakes, and salt flakes, if desired, and serve with sliced bell peppers, if desired. Serve the sauce on the side. 5. Store leftovers in an airtight container in the fridge for up to 4 days or in the freezer for up to a month. Reheat in a preheated 180°C air fryer for 3 minutes per side, or until heated through.

Chicken Legs With Leeks

Servings: 6
Cooking Time: 18 Minutes
Ingredients:

- 2 leeks, sliced
- 2 large-sized tomatoes, chopped
- 3 cloves garlic, minced
- ½ teaspoon dried oregano
- 6 chicken legs, boneless and skinless
- ½ teaspoon smoked cayenne pepper
- 2 tablespoons olive oil
- A freshly ground nutmeg

Directions:

1. In a mixing dish, thoroughly combine all ingredients, minus the leeks. Place in the refrigerator and let it marinate overnight.
2. Lay the leeks onto the bottom of the two air fryer drawers. Top with the chicken legs.
3. Roast chicken legs at 190°C for 18 minutes, turning halfway through. Serve with hoisin sauce.

Chicken And Broccoli

Servings: 4

Cooking Time: 15 Minutes

Ingredients:

- 1-pound boneless, skinless chicken breast or thighs, cut into 1-inch bite-sized pieces
- 1/4 –1/2 pound broccoli, cut into florets (1–2 cups)
- 1/2 medium onion, cut into thick slices
- 3 tablespoons olive oil or grape seed oil
- 1/2 teaspoon garlic powder
- 1 tablespoon fresh minced ginger
- 1 tablespoon low-sodium soy sauce
- 1 tablespoon rice vinegar
- 1 teaspoon sesame oil
- 2 teaspoons hot sauce (optional)
- 1/2 teaspoon sea salt, or to taste
- Black pepper, to taste
- Lemon wedges, for serving (optional)

Directions:

1. Combine the oil, garlic powder, ginger, soy sauce, rice vinegar, sesame oil, optional spicy sauce, salt, and pepper in a large mixing bowl.
2. Put the chicken in a separate bowl.
3. In a separate bowl, combine the broccoli and onions.
4. Divide the marinade between the two bowls and toss to evenly coat each.
5. Install a crisper plate into both drawers. Place the broccoli in the zone 1 drawer, then insert the drawer into the unit. Place the chicken breasts in the zone 2 drawer, then insert the drawer into the unit.
6. Select zone 1, select AIR FRY, set temperature to 390 degrees F/ 200 degrees C, and set time to 10 minutes. Select zone 2, select AIR FRY, set temperature to 390 degrees F/ 200 degrees C, and set time to 20 minutes. Select SYNC. Press the START/STOP button to begin cooking.
7. When zone 2 time reaches 9 minutes, press START/STOP to pause the unit. Remove the drawer and toss the chicken. Re-insert the drawer into the unit and press START/STOP to resume cooking.
8. When cooking is complete, serve the chicken breasts and broccoli while still hot.
9. Add additional salt and pepper to taste. Squeeze optional fresh lemon juice on top and serve warm.

Nutrition:

- (Per serving) Calories 224 | Fat 15.8g | Sodium 203mg | Carbs 4g | Fiber 1g | Sugar 1g | Protein 25g

Chicken & Veggies

Servings: 4
Cooking Time: 10 Minutes

Ingredients:

- 450g chicken breast, boneless & cut into pieces
- 2 garlic cloves, minced
- 15ml olive oil
- 239g frozen mix vegetables
- 1 tbsp Italian seasoning
- ½ tsp chilli powder
- ½ tsp garlic powder
- Pepper
- Salt

Directions:

1. In a bowl, toss chicken with remaining ingredients until well coated.
2. Insert a crisper plate in the Tower air fryer baskets.
3. Add chicken and vegetables in both baskets.
4. Select zone 1 then select "air fry" mode and set the temperature to 390 degrees F for 10 minutes. Press "match" to match zone 2 settings to zone 1. Press "start/stop" to begin.

Nutrition:

- (Per serving) Calories 221 | Fat 7.6g |Sodium 126mg | Carbs 10.6g | Fiber 3.3g | Sugar 2.7g | Protein 26.3g

Glazed Thighs With French Fries

Servings:3
Cooking Time:35

Ingredients:

- 2 tablespoons of Soy Sauce
- Salt, to taste
- 1 teaspoon of Worcestershire Sauce
- 2 teaspoons Brown Sugar
- 1 teaspoon of Ginger, paste
- 1 teaspoon of Garlic, paste
- 6 Boneless Chicken Thighs
- 1 pound of hand-cut potato fries
- 2 tablespoons of canola oil

Directions:

1. Coat the French fries well with canola oil.
2. Season it with salt.
3. In a small bowl, combine the soy sauce, Worcestershire sauce, brown sugar, ginger, and garlic.
4. Place the chicken in this marinade and let it sit for 40 minutes.
5. Put the chicken thighs into the zone 1 basket and fries into the zone 2 basket.
6. Press button 1 for the first basket, and set it to ROAST mode at 350 degrees F for 35 minutes.
7. For the second basket hit 2 and set time to 30 minutes at 360 degrees F, by selecting AIR FRY mode.
8. Once the cooking cycle completely take out the fries and chicken and serve it hot.

Nutrition:

- (Per serving) Calories 858| Fat39g | Sodium 1509mg | Carbs 45.6g | Fiber 4.4g | Sugar3 g | Protein 90g

Sweet-and-sour Chicken With Pineapple Cauliflower Rice

Servings: 4
Cooking Time: 30 Minutes

Ingredients:

- FOR THE CHICKEN
- ¼ cup cornstarch, plus 2 teaspoons
- ¼ teaspoon kosher salt
- 2 large eggs
- 1 tablespoon sesame oil
- 1½ pounds boneless, skinless chicken breasts, cut into 1-inch pieces
- Nonstick cooking spray
- 6 tablespoons ketchup
- ¾ cup apple cider vinegar
- 1½ tablespoons soy sauce
- 1 tablespoon sugar
- FOR THE CAULIFLOWER RICE
- 1 cup finely diced fresh pineapple
- 1 red bell pepper, thinly sliced
- 1 small red onion, thinly sliced
- 1 tablespoon vegetable oil
- 2 cups frozen cauliflower rice, thawed
- 2 tablespoons soy sauce
- 1 teaspoon sesame oil
- 2 scallions, sliced

Directions:

1. To prep the chicken:
2. Set up a breading station with two small shallow bowls. Combine ¼ cup of cornstarch and the salt in the first bowl. In the second bowl, beat the eggs with the sesame oil.
3. Dip the chicken pieces in the cornstarch mixture to coat, then into the egg mixture, then back into the cornstarch mixture to coat. Mist the coated pieces with cooking spray.
4. In a small bowl, whisk together the ketchup, vinegar, soy sauce, sugar, and remaining 2 teaspoons of cornstarch.
5. To prep the cauliflower rice: Blot the pineapple dry with a paper towel. In a large bowl, combine the pineapple, bell pepper, onion, and vegetable oil.
6. To cook the chicken and cauliflower rice: Install a crisper plate in each of the two baskets. Place the chicken in the Zone 1 basket and insert the basket in the unit. Place a piece of aluminum foil over the crisper plate in the Zone 2 basket and add the pineapple mixture. Insert the basket in the unit.
7. Select Zone 1, select AIR FRY, set the temperature to 400°F, and set the time to 30 minutes.
8. Select Zone 2, select AIR BROIL, set the temperature to 450°F, and set the time to 12 minutes. Select SMART FINISH.
9. Press START/PAUSE to begin cooking.
10. When the Zone 2 timer reads 4 minutes, press START/PAUSE. Remove the basket and stir in the cauliflower rice, soy sauce, and sesame oil. Reinsert the basket and press START/PAUSE to resume cooking.
11. When cooking is complete, the chicken will be golden brown and cooked through and the rice warmed through. Stir the scallions into the rice and serve.

African Piri-piri Chicken Drumsticks

Servings: 2
Cooking Time: 20 Minutes
Ingredients:

- Chicken:
- 1 tablespoon chopped fresh thyme leaves
- 1 tablespoon minced fresh ginger
- 1 small shallot, finely chopped
- 2 garlic cloves, minced
- 80 ml piri-piri sauce or hot sauce
- 3 tablespoons extra-virgin olive oil
- Zest and juice of 1 lemon
- 1 teaspoon smoked paprika
- ½ teaspoon kosher salt
- ½ teaspoon black pepper
- 4 chicken drumsticks
- Glaze:
- 2 tablespoons butter or ghee
- 1 teaspoon chopped fresh thyme leaves
- 1 garlic clove, minced
- 1 tablespoon piri-piri sauce
- 1 tablespoon fresh lemon juice

Directions:

1. For the chicken: In a small bowl, stir together all the ingredients except the chicken. Place the chicken and the marinade in a gallon-size resealable plastic bag. Seal the bag and massage to coat. Refrigerate for at least 2 hours or up to 24 hours, turning the bag occasionally. 2. Place the chicken legs in the zone 1 air fryer basket. Set the air fryer to 200°C for 20 minutes, turning the chicken halfway through the cooking time. 3. Meanwhile, for the glaze: Melt the butter in a small saucepan over medium-high heat. Add the thyme and garlic. Cook, stirring, until the garlic just begins to brown, 1 to 2 minutes. Add the piri-piri sauce and lemon juice. Reduce the heat to medium-low and simmer for 1 to 2 minutes. 4. Transfer the chicken to a serving platter. Pour the glaze over the chicken. Serve immediately.

Bacon Wrapped Stuffed Chicken

Servings: 4
Cooking Time: 25 Minutes
Ingredients:

- 3 boneless chicken breasts
- 6 jalapenos, sliced
- ¾ cup (170g) cream cheese
- ½ cup Monterey Jack cheese, shredded
- 1 teaspoon ground cumin
- 12 strips thick bacon

Directions:

1. Cut the chicken breasts in half crosswise and pound them with a mallet.
2. Mix cream cheese with cumin and Monterey jacket cheese in a bowl.
3. Spread the cream cheese mixture over the chicken breast slices.
4. Add jalapeno slices on top and wrap the chicken slices.
5. Wrap each chicken rolls with a bacon slice.
6. Place the wrapped rolls into the Tower 2 Baskets Air Fryer baskets.
7. Return the air fryer basket 1 to Zone 1, and basket 2 to Zone 2 of the Tower 2-Basket Air Fryer.
8. Choose the “Air Fry” mode for Zone 1 at 340 degrees F and 25 minutes of cooking time.
9. Select the “MATCH COOK” option to copy the settings for Zone 2.
10. Initiate cooking by pressing the START/PAUSE BUTTON.
11. Serve warm.

Nutrition:

- (Per serving) Calories 220 | Fat 1.7g |Sodium 178mg | Carbs 1.7g | Fiber 0.2g | Sugar 0.2g | Protein 32.9g

Bang-bang Chicken

Servings: 2
Cooking Time: 20 Minutes

Ingredients:

- 1 cup mayonnaise
- ½ cup sweet chili sauce
- 2 tablespoons Sriracha sauce
- ⅓ cup flour
- 1 lb. boneless chicken breast, diced
- 1 ½ cups panko bread crumbs
- 2 green onions, chopped

Directions:

1. Mix mayonnaise with Sriracha and sweet chili sauce in a large bowl.
2. Keep ¾ cup of the mixture aside.
3. Add flour, chicken, breadcrumbs, and remaining mayo mixture to a resealable plastic bag.
4. Zip the bag and shake well to coat.
5. Divide the chicken in the two crisper plates in a single layer.
6. Return the crisper plate to the Tower Dual Zone Air Fryer.
7. Choose the Air Fry mode for Zone 1 and set the temperature to 390 degrees F and the time to 20 minutes|
8. Select the "MATCH" button to copy the settings for Zone 2.
9. Initiate cooking by pressing the START/STOP button.
10. Flip the chicken once cooked halfway through.
11. Top the chicken with reserved mayo sauce.
12. Garnish with green onions and serve warm.

Lemon Thyme Roasted Chicken

Servings: 6
Cooking Time: 60 Minutes

Ingredients:

- 2 tablespoons baking powder
- 1 teaspoon smoked paprika
- Sea salt and freshly ground black pepper, to taste
- 900 g chicken wings or chicken drumettes
- Avocado oil spray
- 80 ml avocado oil
- 120 ml Buffalo hot sauce, such as Frank's RedHot
- 4 tablespoons unsalted butter
- 2 tablespoons apple cider vinegar
- 1 teaspoon minced garlic

Directions:

1. In a large bowl, stir together the baking powder, smoked paprika, and salt and pepper to taste. Add the chicken wings and toss to coat.
2. Set the air fryer to 200°C. Spray the wings with oil.
3. Place the wings in the two drawers in a single layer and air fry for 20 to 25 minutes. Check with an instant-read thermometer and remove when they reach 70°C. Let rest until they reach 76°C.
4. While the wings are cooking, whisk together the avocado oil, hot sauce, butter, vinegar, and garlic in a small saucepan over medium-low heat until warm.
5. When the wings are done cooking, toss them with the Buffalo sauce. Serve warm.

Desserts Recipes

Homemade Mini Cheesecake

Servings: 2
Cooking Time: 15 Minutes
Ingredients:

- ½ cup walnuts
- 2 tablespoons salted butter
- 2 tablespoons granular erythritol
- 4 ounces full-fat cream cheese, softened
- 1 large egg
- ½ teaspoon vanilla extract
- ⅛ cup powdered erythritol

Directions:

1. Place butter, granular erythritol, and walnuts in a food processor. Pulse until all the ingredients stick together to form a dough.
2. Place dough into 4&quot| springform pan then put the pan into the air fryer basket.
3. Set the temperature to 400°F, then set the timer for 5 minutes.
4. When timer goes off, remove the crust and allow it rest.
5. Stir cream cheese with vanilla extract, powdered erythritol and egg until smooth in a medium bowl.
6. Pour mixture on top of baked walnut crust and then put into the air fryer basket.
7. Set the temperature to 300°F, then set the timer for 10 minutes.
8. Once cooked fully, allow to cool for 2 hours before serving.

Air Fryer Sweet Twists

Servings: 2
Cooking Time: 10 Minutes
Ingredients:

- 1 box store-bought puff pastry
- ½ teaspoon cinnamon
- ½ teaspoon sugar
- ½ teaspoon black sesame seeds
- Salt, pinch
- 2 tablespoons Parmesan cheese, freshly grated

Directions:

1. Place the dough on a work surface.
2. Take a small bowl and mix in cheese, sugar, salt, sesame seeds, and cinnamon.
3. Press this mixture on both sides of the dough.
4. Now, cut the pastry into 1" x 3" strips.
5. Twist each of the strips twice from each end.
6. Transfer them to both the air fryer baskets.
7. Select zone 1 to AIR FRY mode at 400 degrees F for 9-10 minutes.
8. Select the MATCH button for the zone 2 basket.
9. Once cooked, serve.

Pumpkin Hand Pies Blueberry Hand Pies

Servings:4
Cooking Time: 15 Minutes

Ingredients:

- FOR THE PUMPKIN HAND PIES
- ½ cup pumpkin pie filling (from a 15-ounce can)
- ⅓ cup half-and-half
- 1 large egg
- ½ refrigerated pie crust (from a 14.1-ounce package)
- 1 large egg yolk
- 1 tablespoon whole milk
- FOR THE BLUEBERRY HAND PIES
- ¼ cup blueberries
- 2 tablespoons granulated sugar
- 1 tablespoon grated lemon zest (optional)
- ¼ teaspoon cornstarch
- 1 teaspoon fresh lemon juice
- ⅛ teaspoon kosher salt
- ½ refrigerated pie crust (from a 14.1-ounce package)
- 1 large egg yolk
- 1 tablespoon whole milk
- ½ teaspoon turbinado sugar

Directions:

1. To prep the pumpkin hand pies: In a small bowl, mix the pumpkin pie filling, half-and-half, and whole egg until well combined and smooth.
2. Cut the dough in half to form two wedges. Divide the pumpkin pie filling between the wedges. Fold the crust over to completely encase the filling. Using a fork, crimp the edges, forming a tight seal.
3. In a small bowl, whisk together the egg yolk and milk. Brush over the pastry. Carefully cut two small vents in the top of each pie.
4. To prep the blueberry hand pies: In a small bowl, combine the blueberries, granulated sugar, lemon zest (if using), cornstarch, lemon juice, and salt.
5. Cut the dough in half to form two wedges. Divide the blueberry filling between the wedges. Fold the crust over to completely encase the filling. Using a fork, crimp the edges, forming a tight seal.
6. In a small bowl, whisk together the egg yolk and milk. Brush over the pastry. Sprinkle with the turbinado sugar. Carefully cut two small vents in the top of each pie.
7. To cook the hand pies: Install a crisper plate in each of the two baskets. Place the pumpkin hand pies in the Zone 1 basket and insert the basket in the unit. Place the blueberry hand pies in the Zone 2 basket and insert the basket in the unit.
8. Select Zone 1, select AIR FRY, set the temperature to 350°F, and set the timer to 15 minutes. Select MATCH COOK to match Zone 2 settings to Zone 1.
9. Press START/PAUSE to begin cooking.
10. When cooking is complete, the pie crust should be crisp and golden brown and the filling bubbling.
11. Let the hand pies cool for at least 30 minutes before serving.

Nutrition:

- (Per serving) Calories: 588; Total fat: 33g; Saturated fat: 14g; Carbohydrates: 68g; Fiber: 0.5g; Protein: 10g; Sodium: 583mg

Mocha Pudding Cake Vanilla Pudding Cake

Servings:8
Cooking Time: 25 Minutes
Ingredients:

- FOR THE MOCHA PUDDING CAKE
- 1 cup all-purpose flour
- ⅔ cup granulated sugar
- 1 cup packed light brown sugar, divided
- 5 tablespoons unsweetened cocoa powder, divided
- 2 teaspoons baking powder
- ¼ teaspoon kosher salt
- ½ cup unsweetened almond milk
- 2 teaspoons vanilla extract
- 2 tablespoons vegetable oil
- 1 cup freshly brewed coffee
- FOR THE VANILLA PUDDING CAKE
- 1 cup all-purpose flour
- ⅔ cup granulated sugar, plus ½ cup
- 2 teaspoons baking powder
- ¼ teaspoon kosher salt
- ½ cup unsweetened almond milk
- 2½ teaspoons vanilla extract, divided
- 2 tablespoons vegetable oil
- ¾ cup hot water
- 2 teaspoons cornstarch

Directions:

1. To prep the mocha pudding cake: In a medium bowl, combine the flour, granulated sugar, ½ cup of brown sugar, 3 tablespoons of cocoa powder, the baking powder, and salt. Stir in the almond milk, vanilla, and oil to form a thick batter.
2. Spread the batter in the bottom of the Zone 1 basket. Sprinkle the remaining ½ cup brown sugar and 2 tablespoons of cocoa powder in an even layer over the batter. Gently pour the hot coffee over the batter (do not mix).
3. To prep the vanilla pudding cake: In a medium bowl, combine the flour, ⅔ cup of granulated sugar, the baking powder, and salt. Stir in the almond milk, 2 teaspoons of vanilla, and the oil to form a thick batter.
4. Spread the batter in the bottom of the Zone 2 basket.
5. In a small bowl, whisk together the hot water, cornstarch, and remaining ½ cup of sugar and ½ teaspoon of vanilla. Gently pour over the batter (do not mix).
6. To cook both pudding cakes: Insert both baskets in the unit.
7. Select Zone 1, select BAKE, set the temperature to 330°F, and set the timer to 25 minutes. Select MATCH COOK to match Zone 2 settings to Zone 1.
8. Press START/PAUSE to begin cooking.
9. When cooking is complete, the tops of the cakes should be dry and set.
10. Let the cakes rest for 10 minutes before serving. The pudding will thicken as it cools.

Nutrition:

- (Per serving) Calories: 531; Total fat: 8g; Saturated fat: 1g; Carbohydrates: 115g; Fiber: 3.5g; Protein: 5g; Sodium: 111mg

Cinnamon Bread Twists

Servings: 4
Cooking Time: 15 Minutes
Ingredients:

- Bread Twists Dough
- 120g all-purpose flour
- 1 teaspoon baking powder
- ¼ teaspoon salt
- 150g fat free Greek yogurt
- Brushing
- 2 tablespoons light butter
- 2 tablespoons granulated sugar
- 1-2 teaspoons ground cinnamon, to taste

Directions:

1. Mix flour, salt and baking powder in a bowl.
2. Stir in yogurt and the rest of the dough ingredients in a bowl.
3. Mix well and make 8 inches long strips out of this dough.
4. Twist the strips and place them in the air fryer baskets.
5. Return the air fryer basket 1 to Zone 1, and basket 2 to Zone 2 of the Tower 2-Basket Air Fryer.
6. Choose the "Air Fry" mode for Zone 1 at 375 degrees F and 15 minutes of cooking time.
7. Select the "MATCH COOK" option to copy the settings for Zone 2.
8. Initiate cooking by pressing the START/PAUSE BUTTON.
9. Flip the twists once cooked halfway through.
10. Mix butter with cinnamon and sugar in a bowl.
11. Brush this mixture over the twists.
12. Serve.

Nutrition:

- (Per serving) Calories 391 | Fat 24g |Sodium 142mg | Carbs 38.5g | Fiber 3.5g | Sugar 21g | Protein 6.6g

Funnel Cake

Servings: 4
Cooking Time: 5 Minutes
Ingredients:

- Coconut, or avocado oil, for spraying
- 110 g self-raising flour, plus more for dusting
- 240 ml fat-free vanilla Greek yogurt
- ½ teaspoon ground cinnamon
- ¼ cup icing sugar

Directions:

1. Preheat the air fryer to 192°C. Line the two air fryer drawers with baking paper, and spray lightly with oil.
2. In a large bowl, mix together the flour, yogurt and cinnamon until the mixture forms a ball.
3. Place the dough on a lightly floured work surface and knead for about 2 minutes.
4. Cut the dough into 4 equal pieces, then cut each of those into 6 pieces. You should have 24 pieces in total.
5. Roll the pieces into 8- to 10-inch-long ropes. Loosely mound the ropes into 4 piles of 6 ropes.
6. Place the dough piles in the two prepared drawers, and spray liberally with oil.
7. Cook for 5 minutes, or until lightly browned.
8. Dust with the icing sugar before serving.

Biscuit Doughnuts

Servings: 8
Cooking Time: 15 Minutes
Ingredients:

- ½ cup white sugar
- 1 teaspoon cinnamon
- ½ cup powdered sugar
- 1 can pre-made biscuit dough
- Coconut oil
- Melted butter to brush biscuits

Directions:

1. Place all the biscuits on a cutting board and cut holes in the center of each biscuit using a cookie cutter.
2. Grease the crisper plate with coconut oil.
3. Place the biscuits in the two crisper plates while keeping them 1 inch apart.
4. Return the crisper plates to the Tower Dual Zone Air Fryer.
5. Choose the Air Fry mode for Zone 1 and set the temperature to 375 degrees F and the time to 15 minutes.
6. Select the "MATCH" button to copy the settings for Zone 2.
7. Initiate cooking by pressing the START/STOP button.
8. Brush all the donuts with melted butter and sprinkle cinnamon and sugar on top.
9. Air fry these donuts for one minute more.
10. Enjoy!

Cinnamon Sugar Dessert Fries

Servings: 4
Cooking Time: 15 Minutes
Ingredients:

- 2 sweet potatoes
- 1 tablespoon butter, melted
- 1 teaspoon butter, melted
- 2 tablespoons sugar
- ½ teaspoon ground cinnamon

Directions:

1. Peel and cut the sweet potatoes into skinny fries.
2. Coat the fries with 1 tablespoon of butter.
3. Install a crisper plate into each drawer. Place half the sweet potatoes in the zone 1 drawer and half in zone 2's, then insert the drawers into the unit.
4. Select zone 1, select AIR FRY, set temperature to 390°F, and set time to 15 minutes. Select MATCH to match zone 2 settings to zone 1. Press the START/STOP button to begin cooking.
5. When the time reaches 11 minutes, press START/STOP to pause the unit. Remove the drawers and flip the fries. Re-insert the drawers into the unit and press START/STOP to resume cooking.
6. Meanwhile, mix the 1 teaspoon of butter, the sugar, and the cinnamon in a large bowl.
7. When the fries are done, add them to the bowl, and toss them to coat.
8. Serve and enjoy!

Fried Dough With Roasted Strawberries

Servings:4
Cooking Time: 20 Minutes
Ingredients:

- FOR THE FRIED DOUGH
- 6 ounces refrigerated pizza dough, at room temperature
- 2 tablespoons all-purpose flour, for dusting
- 4 tablespoons vegetable oil
- 2 tablespoons powdered sugar
- FOR THE ROASTED STRAWBERRIES
- 2 cups frozen whole strawberries
- 2 tablespoons granulated sugar

Directions:

1. To prep the fried dough: Divide the dough into four equal portions.
2. Dust a clean work surface with the flour. Place one dough portion on the surface and use a rolling pin to roll to a ⅛-inch thickness. Rub both sides of the dough with 1 tablespoon of oil. Repeat with remaining dough portions and oil.
3. To prep the strawberries: Place the strawberries in the Zone 2 basket. Sprinkle the granulated sugar on top.
4. To cook the fried dough and strawberries: Install a crisper plate in the Zone 1 basket. Place 2 dough portions in the basket and insert the basket in the unit. Insert the Zone 2 basket in the unit.
5. Select Zone 1, select AIR FRY, set the temperature to 400°F, and set the timer to 18 minutes.
6. Select Zone 2, select ROAST, set the temperature to 330°F, and set the timer to 20 minutes. Select SMART FINISH.
7. Press START/PAUSE to begin cooking.
8. When both timers read 8 minutes, press START/PAUSE. Remove the Zone 1 basket and transfer the fried dough to a cutting board. Place the 2 remaining dough portions in the basket, then reinsert the basket. Remove the Zone 2 basket and stir the strawberries. Reinsert the basket and press START/PAUSE to resume cooking.
9. When cooking is complete, the dough should be cooked through and the strawberries soft and jammy.
10. Sprinkle the fried dough with powdered sugar. Gently mash the strawberries with a fork. Spoon the strawberries onto each fried dough portion and serve.

Nutrition:

- (Per serving) Calories: 304; Total fat: 15g; Saturated fat: 2.5g; Carbohydrates: 38g; Fiber: 0.5g; Protein: 3g; Sodium: 421mg

Healthy Semolina Pudding

Servings: 4
Cooking Time: 20 Minutes
Ingredients:

- 45g semolina
- 1 tsp vanilla
- 500ml milk
- 115g caster sugar

Directions:

1. Mix semolina and ½ cup milk in a bowl. Slowly add the remaining milk, sugar, and vanilla and mix well.
2. Pour the mixture into four greased ramekins.
3. Insert a crisper plate in the Tower air fryer baskets.
4. Place ramekins in both baskets.
5. Select zone 1, then select "air fry" mode and set the temperature to 300 degrees F for 20 minutes. Press "match" to match zone 2 settings to zone 1. Press "start/stop" to begin.

Nutrition:

- (Per serving) Calories 209 | Fat 2.7g |Sodium 58mg | Carbs 41.5g | Fiber 0.6g | Sugar 30.6g | Protein 5.8g

Mini Peanut Butter Tarts

Servings: 8

Cooking Time: 12 To 15 Minutes

Ingredients:

- 125 g pecans
- 110 g finely ground blanched almond flour
- 2 tablespoons unsalted butter, at room temperature
- 50 g powdered sweetener, plus 2 tablespoons, divided
- 120 g heavy (whipping) cream
- 2 tablespoons mascarpone cheese
- 110 g cream cheese
- 140 g sugar-free peanut butter
- 1 teaspoon pure vanilla extract
- ⅛ teaspoon sea salt
- 85 g organic chocolate chips
- 1 tablespoon coconut oil
- 40 g chopped peanuts or pecans

Directions:

1. Place the pecans in the bowl of a food processor; process until they are finely ground.
2. Transfer the ground pecans to a medium bowl and stir in the almond flour. Add the butter and 2 tablespoons of sweetener and stir until the mixture becomes wet and crumbly.
3. Divide the mixture among 8 silicone muffin cups, pressing the crust firmly with your fingers into the bottom and part way up the sides of each cup.
4. Arrange the muffin cups in the two air fryer drawers. Set the air fryer to 148°C and bake for 12 to 15 minutes, until the crusts begin to brown. Remove the cups from the air fryer and set them aside to cool.
5. In the bowl of a stand mixer, combine the heavy cream and mascarpone cheese. Beat until peaks form. Transfer to a large bowl.
6. In the same stand mixer bowl, combine the cream cheese, peanut butter, remaining 50 g sweetener, vanilla, and salt. Beat at medium-high speed until smooth.
7. Reduce the speed to low and add the heavy cream mixture back a spoonful at a time, beating after each addition.
8. Spoon the peanut butter mixture over the crusts and freeze the tarts for 30 minutes.
9. Place the chocolate chips and coconut oil in the top of a double boiler over high heat. Stir until melted, then remove from the heat.
10. Drizzle the melted chocolate over the peanut butter tarts. Top with the chopped nuts and freeze the tarts for another 15 minutes, until set.
11. Store the peanut butter tarts in an airtight container in the refrigerator for up to 1 week or in the freezer for up to 1 month.

Coconut-custard Pie And Pecan Brownies

Servings: 9

Cooking Time: 20 To 23 Minutes

Ingredients:

- Coconut-Custard Pie:
- 240 ml milk
- 50 g granulated sugar, plus 2 tablespoons
- 30 g scone mix
- 1 teaspoon vanilla extract
- 2 eggs
- 2 tablespoons melted butter
- Cooking spray
- 50 g desiccated, sweetened coconut
- Pecan Brownies:
- 50 g blanched finely ground almond flour
- 55 g powdered sweetener
- 2 tablespoons unsweetened cocoa powder
- ½ teaspoon baking powder
- 55 g unsalted butter, softened
- 1 large egg
- 35 g chopped pecans
- 40 g low-carb, sugar-free chocolate chips

Directions:

1. Make the Coconut-Custard Pie :
2. Place all ingredients except coconut in a medium bowl.
3. Using a hand mixer, beat on high speed for 3 minutes.
4. Let sit for 5 minutes.
5. Preheat the air fryer to 164°C.
6. Spray a baking pan with cooking spray and place pan in the zone 1 air fryer drawer.
7. Pour filling into pan and sprinkle coconut over top.
8. Cook pie for 20 to 23 minutes or until center sets.
9. Make the Pecan Brownies :
10. In a large bowl, mix almond flour, sweetener, cocoa powder, and baking powder. Stir in butter and egg. 2. Fold in pecans and chocolate chips. Scoop mixture into a round baking pan. Place pan into the zone 2 air fryer drawer. 3. Adjust the temperature to 148°C and bake for 20 minutes. 4. When fully cooked a toothpick inserted in center will come out clean. Allow 20 minutes to fully cool and firm up.

"air-fried" Oreos Apple Fries

Servings:4
Cooking Time: 10 Minutes

Ingredients:

- FOR THE "FRIED" OREOS
- 1 teaspoon vegetable oil
- 1 cup all-purpose flour
- 1 tablespoon granulated sugar
- 1 tablespoon baking powder
- ½ teaspoon baking soda
- ¼ teaspoon kosher salt
- 1 large egg
- ¼ cup unsweetened almond milk
- ½ teaspoon vanilla extract
- 8 Oreo cookies
- Nonstick cooking spray
- 1 tablespoon powdered sugar (optional)
- FOR THE APPLE FRIES
- 1 teaspoon vegetable oil
- 1 cup all-purpose flour
- 1 tablespoon granulated sugar
- 1 tablespoon baking powder
- ½ teaspoon baking soda
- ¼ teaspoon kosher salt
- 1 large egg
- ¼ cup unsweetened almond milk
- ½ teaspoon vanilla extract
- 2 Granny Smith apples
- 2 tablespoons cornstarch
- ½ teaspoon apple pie spice
- Nonstick cooking spray
- 1 tablespoon powdered sugar (optional)

Directions:

1. To prep the "fried" Oreos: Brush a crisper plate with the oil and install it in the Zone 1 basket.
2. In a large bowl, combine the flour, granulated sugar, baking powder, baking soda, and salt. Mix in the egg, almond milk, and vanilla to form a thick batter.
3. Using a fork or slotted spoon, dip each cookie into the batter, coating it fully. Let the excess batter drip off, then place the cookies in the prepared basket in a single layer. Spritz each with cooking spray.
4. To prep the apple fries: Brush a crisper plate with the oil and install it in the Zone 2 basket.
5. In a large bowl, combine the flour, granulated sugar, baking powder, baking soda, and salt. Mix in the egg, almond milk, and vanilla to form a thick batter.
6. Core the apples and cut them into ½-inch-thick French fry shapes. Dust lightly with the cornstarch and apple pie spice.
7. Using a fork or slotted spoon, dip each apple into the batter, coating it fully. Let the excess batter drip off, then place the apples in the prepared basket in a single layer. Spritz with cooking spray.
8. To cook the "fried" Oreos and apple fries: Insert both baskets in the unit.
9. Select Zone 1, select AIR FRY, set the temperature to 400°F, and set the timer to 8 minutes.

10. Select Zone 2, select AIR FRY, set the temperature to 400°F, and set the timer to 10 minutes. Select SMART FINISH.
11. Press START/PAUSE to begin cooking.
12. When cooking is complete, the batter will be golden brown and crisp. If desired, dust the cookies and apples with the powdered sugar before serving.

Nutrition:

- (Per serving) Calories: 464; Total fat: 21g; Saturated fat: 3.5g; Carbohydrates: 66g; Fiber: 2.5g; Protein: 7g; Sodium: 293mg

Spiced Apple Cake

Servings: 6
Cooking Time: 30 Minutes

Ingredients:

- Vegetable oil
- 2 diced & peeled Gala apples
- 1 tablespoon fresh lemon juice
- 55 g unsalted butter, softened
- 65 g granulated sugar
- 2 large eggs
- 155 g plain flour
- 1½ teaspoons baking powder
- 1 tablespoon apple pie spice
- ½ teaspoon ground ginger
- ¼ teaspoon ground cardamom
- ¼ teaspoon ground nutmeg
- ½ teaspoon kosher, or coarse sea salt
- 60 ml whole milk
- Icing sugar, for dusting

Directions:

1. Grease a 0.7-liter Bundt, or tube pan with oil; set aside.
2. In a medium bowl, toss the apples with the lemon juice until well coated; set aside.
3. In a large bowl, combine the butter and sugar. Beat with an electric hand mixer on medium speed until the sugar has dissolved. Add the eggs and beat until fluffy. Add the flour, baking powder, apple pie spice, ginger, cardamom, nutmeg, salt, and milk. Mix until the batter is thick but pourable.
4. Pour the batter into the prepared pan. Top batter evenly with the apple mixture. Place the pan in the zone 1 air fryer drawer. Set the temperature to 176°C and cook for 30 minutes, or until a toothpick inserted in the center of the cake comes out clean. Close the air fryer and let the cake rest for 10 minutes. Turn the cake out onto a wire rack and cool completely.
5. Right before serving, dust the cake with icing sugar.

Gluten-free Spice Cookies

Servings: 4
Cooking Time: 12 Minutes
Ingredients:

- 4 tablespoons unsalted butter, at room temperature
- 2 tablespoons agave nectar
- 1 large egg
- 2 tablespoons water
- 240 g almond flour
- 100 g granulated sugar
- 2 teaspoons ground ginger
- 1 teaspoon ground cinnamon
- ½ teaspoon freshly grated nutmeg
- 1 teaspoon baking soda
- ¼ teaspoon kosher, or coarse sea salt

Directions:

1. Line the bottom of the air fryer basket with baking paper cut to fit.
2. In a large bowl, using a hand mixer, beat together the butter, agave, egg, and water on medium speed until light and fluffy.
3. Add the almond flour, sugar, ginger, cinnamon, nutmeg, baking soda, and salt. Beat on low speed until well combined.
4. Roll the dough into 2-tablespoon balls and arrange them on the baking paper in the basket. Set the air fryer to 165°C, and cook for 12 minutes, or until the tops of cookies are lightly browned.
5. Transfer to a wire rack and let cool completely. Store in an airtight container for up to a week.

Lava Cake

Servings: 4
Cooking Time: 15 Minutes
Ingredients:

- 1 cup semi-sweet chocolate chips
- 8 tablespoons butter
- 4 eggs
- 2 teaspoons vanilla extract
- ½ teaspoon salt
- 6 tablespoons all-purpose flour
- 1 cup powdered sugar
- For the chocolate filling:
- 2 tablespoons Nutella
- 1 tablespoon butter, softened
- 1 tablespoon powdered sugar

Directions:

1. Heat the chocolate chips and butter in a medium-sized microwave-safe bowl in 30-second intervals until thoroughly melted and smooth, stirring after each interval.
2. Whisk together the eggs, vanilla, salt, flour, and powdered sugar in a mixing bowl.
3. Combine the Nutella, softened butter, and powdered sugar in a separate bowl.
4. Spray 4 ramekins with oil and fill them halfway with the chocolate chip mixture. Fill each ramekin halfway with Nutella, then top with the remaining chocolate chip mixture, making sure the Nutella is well covered.
5. Install a crisper plate in both drawers. Place 2 ramekins in each drawer and insert the drawers into the unit.
6. Select zone 1, select AIR FRY, set temperature to 390°F, and set time to 22 minutes. Select MATCH to match zone 2 settings to zone 1. Press the START/STOP button to begin cooking.
7. Serve hot.

Apple Pie Rolls

Servings: 8

Cooking Time: 12 Minutes

Ingredients:

- 3 cups tart apples, peeled, cored and chopped
- ½ cup light brown sugar
- 2½ teaspoon ground cinnamon, divided
- 1 teaspoon corn starch
- 8 egg roll wrappers
- ½ cup cream cheese, softened
- Non-stick cooking spray
- 2 tablespoons sugar

Directions:

1. In a small bowl, mix together the apples, brown sugar, 1 teaspoon of cinnamon and corn starch.
2. Arrange 1 egg roll wrapper onto a smooth surface.
3. Spread about 1 tablespoon of cream cheese over roll, leaving 1-inch of edges.
4. Place ⅓ cup of apple mixture over one corner of a wrapper, just below the center.
5. Fold the bottom corner over filling.
6. With wet fingers, moisten the remaining wrapper edges.
7. Fold side corners toward center over the filling.
8. Roll egg roll up tightly and with your fingers, press at tip to seal.
9. Repeat with the remaining wrappers, cream cheese and filling.
10. Spray the rolls with cooking spray evenly.
11. Press "Zone 1" and "Zone 2" and then rotate the knob for each zone to select "Air Fry".
12. Set the temperature to 400 degrees F/ 200 degrees C for both zones and then set the time for 5 minutes to preheat.
13. After preheating, arrange 4 rolls into the basket of each zone.
14. Slide each basket into Air Fryer and set the time for 12 minutes.
15. While cooking, flip the rolls once halfway through and spray with the cooking spray.
16. Meanwhile, in a shallow dish, mix together the sugar and remaining cinnamon.
17. After cooking time is completed, remove the rolls from Air Fryer.
18. Coat the rolls with sugar mixture and serve.

Simple Cheesecake

Servings: 3
Cooking Time: 20 Minutes
Ingredients:

- ½ egg
- 2 tablespoons sugar
- ⅛ teaspoon vanilla extract
- ¼ cup honey graham cracker crumbs
- ½ tablespoon unsalted butter, softened
- ¼ pound cream cheese, softened

Directions:

1. Line a round baking dish with parchment paper.
2. For crust: In a bowl, add the graham cracker crumbs and butter.
3. Place the crust into baking dish and press to smooth.
4. Press "Zone 1" and "Zone 2" and then rotate the knob for each zone to select "Bake".
5. Set the temperature to 350 degrees F/ 175 degrees C for both zones and then set the time for 5 minutes to preheat.
6. After preheating, arrange the baking dish into the basket of each zone.
7. Slide each basket into Air Fryer and set the time for 4 minutes.
8. Remove the crust from the oven and set aside to cool slightly.
9. Meanwhile, take a bowl, add the cream cheese and sugar. Whisk until smooth.
10. Now, place the eggs, one at a time and whisk until mixture becomes creamy.
11. Add the vanilla extract and mix well.
12. Place the cream cheese mixture evenly over the crust.
13. Arrange the baking dish into the Air-Fryer basket.
14. Remove from the oven and set aside to cool.
15. Serve and enjoy!

Simple Pineapple Sticks And Crispy Pineapple Rings

Servings: 9
Cooking Time: 10 Minutes
Ingredients:

- Simple Pineapple Sticks:
- ½ fresh pineapple, cut into sticks
- 25 g desiccated coconut
- Crispy Pineapple Rings:
- 240 ml rice milk
- 85 g plain flour
- 120 ml water
- 25 g unsweetened flaked coconut
- 4 tablespoons granulated sugar
- ½ teaspoon baking soda
- ½ teaspoon baking powder
- ½ teaspoon vanilla essence
- ½ teaspoon ground cinnamon
- ¼ teaspoon ground star anise
- Pinch of kosher, or coarse sea salt

- 1 medium pineapple, peeled and sliced

Directions:

1. Simple Pineapple Sticks :
2. Preheat the air fryer to 204°C.
3. Coat the pineapple sticks in the desiccated coconut and put in the zone 1 air fryer drawer.
4. Air fry for 10 minutes.
5. Serve immediately
6. Crispy Pineapple Rings :
7. Preheat the air fryer to 204°C.
8. In a large bowl, stir together all the ingredients except the pineapple.
9. Dip each pineapple slice into the batter until evenly coated.
10. Arrange the pineapple slices in the zone 2 drawer and air fry for 6 to 8 minutes until golden brown.
11. Remove from the drawer to a plate and cool for 5 minutes before serving warm

Coconut Muffins And Dark Chocolate Lava Cake

Servings: 9
Cooking Time: 25 Minutes

Ingredients:

- Coconut Muffins:
- 55 g coconut flour
- 2 tablespoons cocoa powder
- 3 tablespoons granulated sweetener
- 1 teaspoon baking powder
- 2 tablespoons coconut oil
- 2 eggs, beaten
- 50 g desiccated coconut
- Dark Chocolate Lava Cake:
- Olive oil cooking spray
- 30 g whole wheat flour
- 1 tablespoon unsweetened dark chocolate cocoa powder
- ⅛ teaspoon salt
- ½ teaspoon baking powder
- 60 ml raw honey
- 1 egg
- 2 tablespoons olive oil

Directions:

1. Make the Coconut Muffins :
2. In the mixing bowl, mix all ingredients.
3. Then pour the mixture into the molds of the muffin and transfer in the zone 1 air fryer basket.
4. Cook the muffins at 175°C for 25 minutes.
5. Make the Dark Chocolate Lava Cake :
6. Preheat the air fryer to 190°C. Lightly coat the insides of four ramekins with olive oil cooking spray.
7. In a medium bowl, combine the flour, cocoa powder, salt, baking powder, honey, egg, and olive oil.
8. Divide the batter evenly among the ramekins.
9. Place the filled ramekins inside the zone 2 air fryer basket and bake for 10 minutes.
10. Remove the lava cakes from the air fryer and slide a knife around the outside edge of each cake. Turn each ramekin upside down on a saucer and serve.

RECIPES INDEX

Z

Printed in Great Britain
by Amazon

37387407R00057